PENDLESIDE AND BRONTË COUNTRY
WALKS FOR MOTORISTS

Companion Volumes

NORTH YORK MOORS WALKS FOR MOTORISTS
NORTH AND EAST
WEST AND SOUTH

LAKE DISTRICT WALKS FOR MOTORISTS
WESTERN AREA
NORTHERN AREA
CENTRAL AREA

PEAK DISTRICT WALKS FOR MOTORISTS

YORKSHIRE DALES WALKS FOR MOTORISTS

FURTHER DALES WALKS FOR MOTORISTS

THE DALES WAY

WALKING THE PENNINE WAY

The photographs on the cover show
Pendle Hill and Haworth Village

© 1974 George Banks

ISBN 0 900397 28 4

Several of the photographs are reproduced by courtesy of the Editor of the 'Lancashire Evening Star', to whom we express our thanks

The Publisher

Printed by Galava Printing Co. Ltd., Nelson, Lancashire

PENDLESIDE and BRONTË COUNTRY
WALKS FOR MOTORISTS

30 Circular Walks

by GEORGE BANKS

30 Sketch maps by the author
8 Photographs

1974

GERRARD PUBLICATIONS
6 Edge End Avenue
BRIERFIELD, NELSON, LANCASHIRE

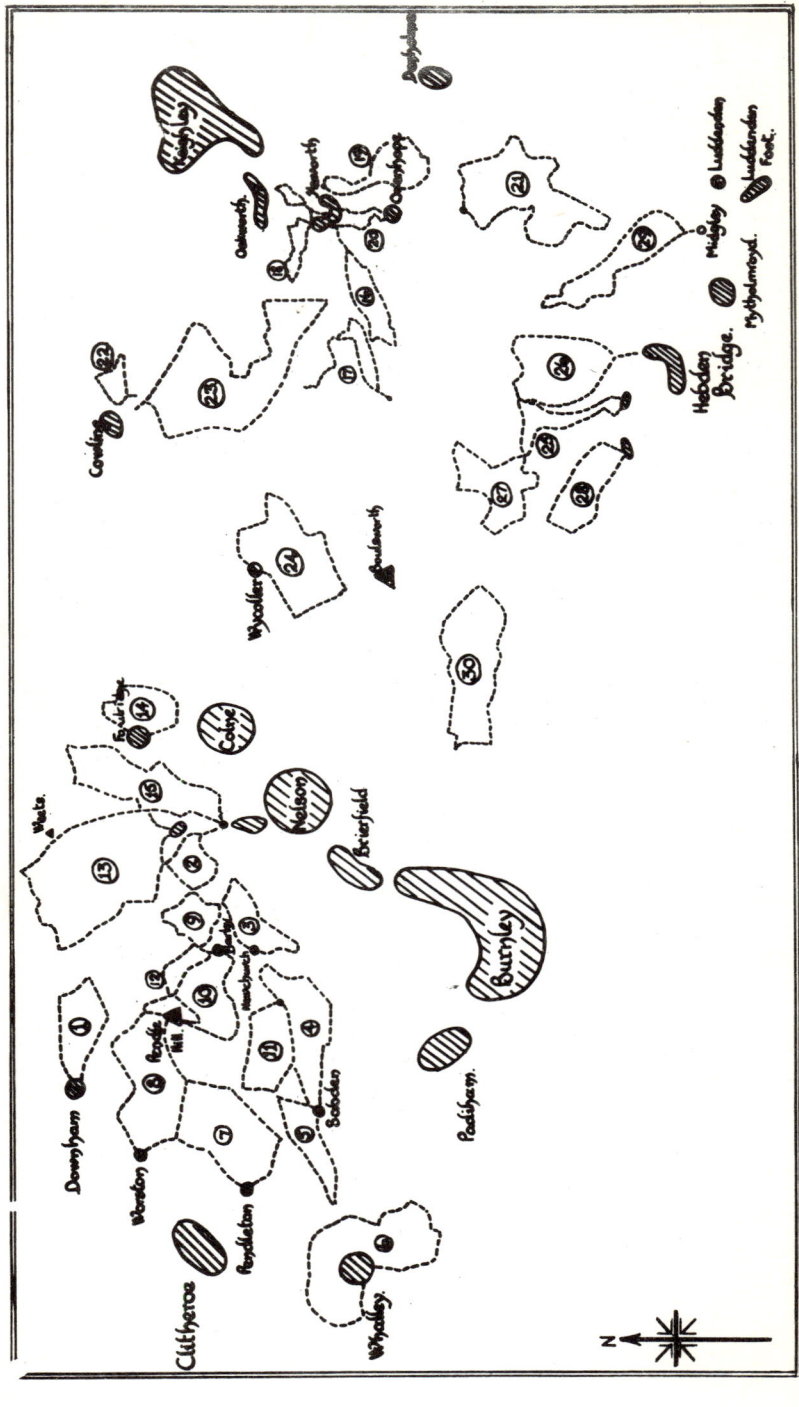

Contents

PENDLESIDE WALKS

1. Twiston and Downham — 9
2. The Water Meetings from Higherford — 13
3. Newchurch and the Noggarth Ridge — 17
4. The Sabden Valley — 21
5. Churn Clough and the Whins from Sabden — 25
6. Whalley Nab and Read Hall — 28
7. Mearley Moor from Pendleton — 32
8. Pendle Hill from Worston — 35
9. The Round of Stang Top from Whitehough — 39
10. Pendle via Whinberry Clough — 42
11. Churn Clough, Spence Moor and Cock Clough — 45
12. The Big End of Pendle from Barley — 48
13. Weets and Wheathead from Blacko — 52
14. Noyna Rocks from Foulridge — 56
15. Whitemoor from Higherford — 59

BRONTE COUNTRY WALKS

16. Penistone Hill and the Bronte Waterfall from Haworth — 63
17. Top Withens from Ponden Hall — 66
18. The River Worth from Haworth — 69
19. Brow Moor and Black Moor — 72
20. Oxenhope, Oakworth and the Worth Valley Railway — 75
21. Oxenhope, Warley and Ovenden Moors — 78
22. Cowling Pinnacles — 82
23. The Hitching Stone, Slipppery Ford and the Pennine Way — 85
24. Foster's Leap and Lumb Spout from Wycoller — 88
25. Hardcastle Crags from Slack Top — 91
26. Walshaw Dean, Lumb Bridge and Crimsworth Dean — 95
27. Alcomden Water and Widdop Moor from Blake Dean — 98
28. Reaps Cross and the Pennine Way from Colden — 102
29. The Limer's Way over Midgley Moor — 105
30. Widdop Cross from Swinden Bridge — 109

Introduction

LONG ago, almost before time itself, the area we now call Pendle-side and Bronte country existed as a shallow inland sea. The climate was hot and dry, and life in the sea was abundant. Limestone deposits, made up largely from the shells of dead animal life, were compressed into rock of immense thickness. This rock is known locally as Mountain Limestone. As the sea shallowed and the climate changed, sediments of grit and sand washed down by rivers from a land mass to the north, covered the limestone. Swampy conditions emerged with huge river deltas on which grew gigantic tree-like ferns. This was the beginning of the Coal Measure Period, when dead vegetation decayed and was compressed by successive layers into coal seams.

Towards the end of this quiescent era of geological time, the Earth's crust, thin in parts, began to erupt. Titanic forces split the rocks assunder forcing them up and over others in a gigantic mountain building period. The centre of this seismic thunder was situated at a great distance from this district, yet the ripples of its energy were sufficient to bend the strata into a large dome. This dome was later known as the Pennine Chain.

Now that the rock was above water the agents of weathering began to sculpture it. Glaciers scoured it; rivers, rain and wind shaped it, until it emerged as we see it today, a corner of England without peer. It is like a jewel with a beauty of its own, and just as a pearl has a lustre and sheen which reveals its quality, so this area must be sampled in order to reveal its charm.

Pendle dominates the surrounding country having a character of its own, yet Boulsworth and the Pennine moors, known as Bronte country, have no less a majesty. The walks described within this guide are for those who wish to taste the bitter tang of the peaty uplands or the sweet changing nature of the valleys. They are aimed at the motorist who wishes to stretch his legs rather than the dedicated walker. They cover distances of approximately 4-9 miles in a circular route, on recognised Rights of Way, so that a car can be used as a base. Some are of an easy nature, more in the role of an 'amble', and suitable for a family with youngish children; whilst others demand some effort and cover more strenuous ground. At the beginning of each walk I have used a grading scheme which I set out below.

1. Easy—4-5 miles in length.
2. Moderate—5-7 miles in length possibly with some hilly terrain.
3. Strenuous—7-9 miles—longer, often covering rough country sometimes steep and hilly.

As well as this grading I have given the approximate distances and time to be allowed for each walk.

I would remind all walkers to observe the Country Code, especially with regards to litter and gates, and I would suggest that if you have a dog that some authority is exercised over it when passing near to farm livestock. On my exploratory travels I have conversed with many farmers and have found them to be most co-operative. Not one of them rejected the thought that walkers may be soon be using some of the paths which I have described. Some even stated that it would be pleasant to see walkers crossing some of these now little used paths, and that they had no objection to genuine ramblers but would be against anyone who cause damage. Should you lose the path then keep to the hedge, fence or wall until you find a way out of the field.

Armed with these common-sense rules, I must now say something about equipment. It is almost unnecessary to use an Ordnance Survey map as the sketch maps and description are sufficiently detailed if followed carefully. However, for those who enjoy the use of a map to pick out routes and landmarks the area is fully covered by the 1″ to 1 mile Blackburn/Burnley Sheet No. 95. More detail may be obtained by using the 2½″ to 1 mile series though a number of these are required to cover the area.

It is sensible to wear suitable footwear, though this does not necessarily mean boots. Good waterproof shoes are quite adequate, providing they have a ridged sole, for most of the walks. Some of the moorland and upland routes however may require more support around the ankle but this will be indicated at the beginning of each walk.

Simple lightweight waterproofs should always be carried as Pendleside enjoys the prospect of rain when Pendle is clear, and it is sure to be raining when it is enshrouded in cloud.

Other equipment can be taken at the discretion and requirement of the walker. Remember that though you may have sandwiches in your car, it might be advisable to carry some food, especially in wintertime. I have a passion for winter when the crisp snow and clear atmosphere add a completely new dimension. On these occasions one must adapt ones clothing, carry an extra sweater, have sufficient food in one's rucksac, and inform someone of the route you mean to take and stick to it.

Pendle Hill divides two basic geographical types of land. On the east and south are the soft, lush valleys of Sabden and Roughlea; the heart of the infamous 'witch' country; whilst further east still, long narrow cloughs make indentations into the Bronte country around Ponden and Wycoller. To the west and north of Pendle, limestone begins to appear with its characteristic short grass and white rocky outcrops around Clitheroe, Bolton by Bowland and Twiston.

7

Pendle itself is a brooding giant capped with a band of hard sandstone which dominates the area and also its weather. Its summit is wide and flat with great peat hags that store the moisture precipitated on it, so that Pendle Water which cascades down Ogden Clough rarely if ever runs dry.

Further east, in Bronte country, the wild moors stretch out towards Yorkshire presenting a dour bleak landscape which can be most inhospitable. Walking here in wet weather is one of urgent effort and grim determination. Yet in spite of this character it has an appeal which cannot be denied, for on a clear summer's day when the cotton grass is waving gently in the breeze there is no better walk than that from Widdop via Withins to Ponden, the ghosts of Heathcliffe and Jane Eyre striding out with you.

Each season sees a change in Nature and these can only be appreciated if you go out to see them. The crunch of snow and crackle of ice underfoot, and the soft zephyr winds of summer rippling a field of hay cost nothing except the effort one has to make to see them. No one could remain unaffected by a field completely alive with Lapwing chicks, hiding and scurrying for cover as you stride out over Noggarth ridge in Spring time. Or you may be lucky and start a small herd of Roe Deer close by Bolton by Bowland or Gisburn. Or perhaps on a cold winter's morn as you wallow knee deep in drifts over Pendle, and your aching lungs discharge smoke signals of distress in the cold frosty air, you will come to realise the wonderful sense of peace and satisfaction which is the lot of the lone walker.

In this modern life of worry, strife and toil, there is ever a need for escapism. Many find this in various pursuits such a Golf, Football, Television, Decorating and such; but I wonder if these are as satisfying to the soul as the simple delights I have tried to portray. An appreciation of Nature, the comradeship felt whilst silently sharing a flask of coffee on Weets Hill as the sun slowly sinks over Bowland, and the relaxation of tension are the true values by which men should live. This above all I know to be true and so with these thoughts may I now encourage you to turn the page and try the first excursion in Living.

PENDLESIDE WALKS

I HAVE chosen Downham village as the start to the first walk in this guide, as it is a centre known to all local people. Downham Hall is the country residence of Lord Clitheroe, and the lands surrounding it belong to his family. As a village it is renowned as one of the prettiest in the north of England, and as such in summertime it is the focus of the weekend motorist. They descend on it in their hundreds to park on the green, eat ice cream, and paddle in the stream until the village takes on the atmosphere of a tourist centre. Few of them, however, stretch their legs further than a walk up the main street and a wander round the quaint and delightful church, so that the walk described will take you away from the maddening crowds.

Walk 1   Twiston and Downham

Grade—Easy walking—stout shoes quite adequate.
Distance—approximately 4 miles.
Time—allow 2 to 3 hours.

THERE are some walks that you never forget and this is one of them. I first strode along its gentle paths as a boy and remember every inch of the way. The gradients are gentle and the variety of the terrain captures your interest all the way round, for some of the views are quite extraordinary in spite of this being only a valley walk. Nowadays with footpaths not being used as much as they used to be some of the paths are overgrown and route finding could be difficult, but if the directions are closely followed you will not stray.

The only car park in the village is that belonging to the Assheton Arms. Near to the bridge is an unofficial layby where you may park, though the green is often used on payment of a fee at weekends. Having left your car at some convenient point in the village make your way to the small bridge, the only one, crossing Downham Beck. This is your starting point.

From here you may optimistically stride out on either side of the stream against the current until you are forced across a small footbridge if you are on the left bank, and eventually arrive at the end of the road. The path goes through the stile and follows Downham Beck for about 100 yards before striking out to the right. Ignoring a track, which leads directly across open country to a gate in a fence, set your sights on a tall tree and the corner of the field where you will find a stile over a fence besides a small tributary brook of Downham Beck.

Keeping the brook on your lefthand side, cross two stiles and then make your way directly into a small copse of trees. On entering this shaded area you will see a footbridge taking you over to the lefthand side of the brook. The path now follows a fence on your

9

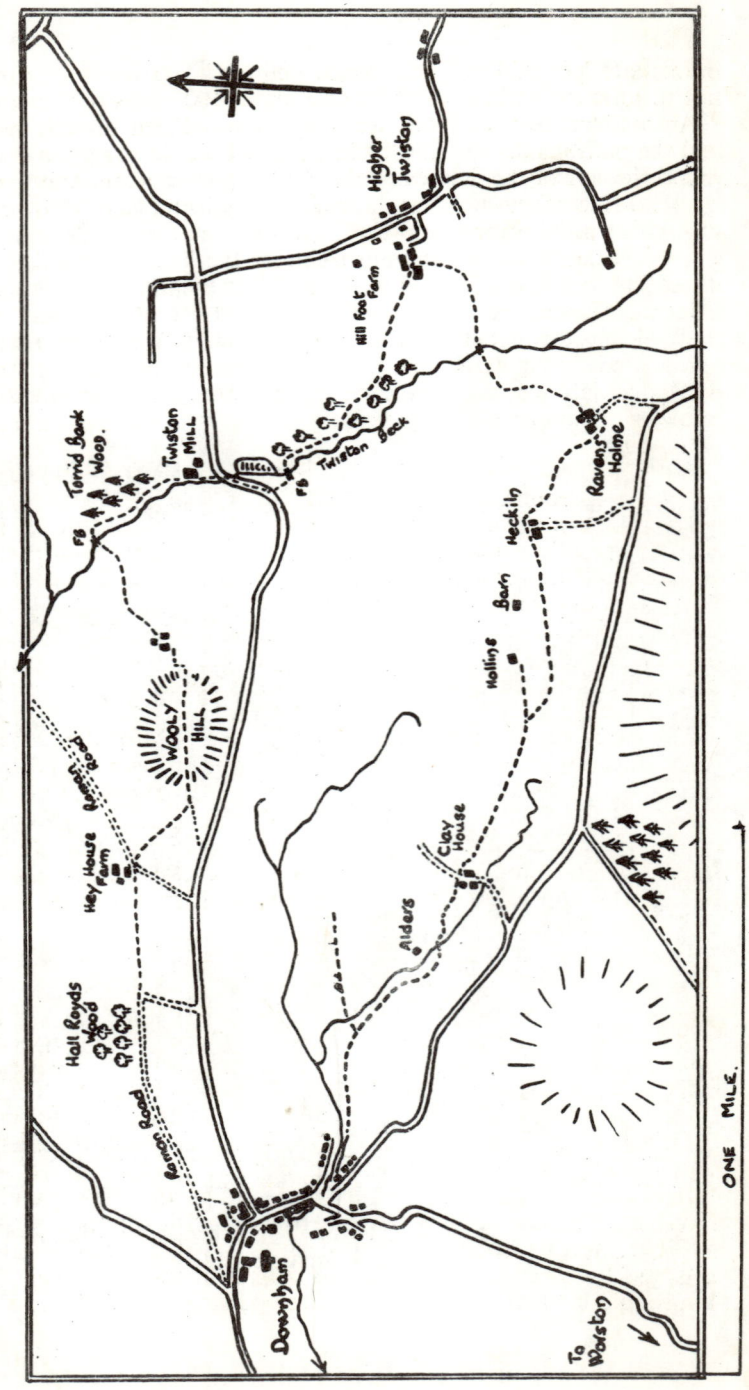

Downham — Twiston

One Mile.

immediate left, still in this wooded dell, and you must be carefu not to miss the rather indistinct stile about 100 yards further on.

Across this stile you will see Clay House Farm directly ahead and the path makes straight for it, though I would suggest a detour round the side of the field when the hay crop is growing. Aim for the lefthand side of the buildings and go through the gate, or over the stile in the wall into the farm yard. Turn left, and proceed round the side of the last building on your right. At the back of it make your way towards a line of trees for about a quarter of a mile, crossing a fence and eventually arriving at a stone wall with a stile in it. Two tracks lead off from here, one following the wallside towards Hollins, and the other, the easier one to follow, crosses the stile and strikes out to the left across rough pasture. This one leads to a stone stile crossing the unmetalled road linking Hollins with the main road on your right.

Straight ahead of you lies Hecklin Farm with a barn slightly on your left, both surrounded by trees. Make your way alongside a fence which dips to a stone wall and stile. Cross the brook and muddy area, then up the other side to arrive at Hecklin across an open pasture. Go through the farmyard and the last gate on your lefthand side. Turn right and follow the side of the building uphill towards some tall trees. Follow them as they curve to the left carefully searching the hedgerow from a rather concealed gate besides which is a wooden stile. On passing through this stile keep the hedge on your lefthand side and make your way directly to Ravens House Farm.

The iron gate at the end of the field to the right of the buildings leads onto an unmetalled road. Follow this through the farmyard taking the first gate on your right between buildings into a field. Turn left and follow the fence and hedge downhill to the bottom corner of the field where a stile is crossed. Now keep on the righthand side of a fence and continue downwards crossing the contours to a narrow concealed exit from the field leading to the upper reaches of Twiston Beck.

Here should be a footbridge but it has long since disappeared. Instead of crossing the beck at this point where the bank is steep and awkward follow downstream until you come across a 4 foot wide gate. Go through this and cross the beck. Climb out of the valley on your right going slightly upstream until you meet a fence. Follow this fence uphill to a gate on your right, turn left however, and pick up a track which takes you directly into Twiston at Hill Foot Farm.

Opposite the farm are three cottages where the weary traveller can obtain a cup of tea and sustenance for the remainder of his walk. 'Mrs Tarns' is a bye-word to rambling groups and cycling clubs in Northern England and it is rare that you will visit here of a weekend without meeting some kindred spirit. Mrs Tarn was a school-mistress living in retirement in this delightful spot, who kept open house and a warm welcome to anyone passing that way. As a boy,

11

during the last war, I visited her cottage many times to eat my sandwiches, drink a cup of tea, and dry my steaming anorak in front of her black leaded firegrate. When she died her passing was mourned by hundreds of walkers and cyclists from all over the North and her memory is revered by them. She stood for the real values that finally matter in this materialistic life of ours, and I am pleased to say that her daughter is continuing this tradition.

Leave Hill Foot Farm through the farmyard via a gate, and cross onto the limestone of Hill Top. Skirt this knoll on a grassy sward until your route begins to drop downhill. The 'big-end' of Pendle is magnificent on your left, and the distant Bowland escarpment ring your views ahead. The immediate scenery changes from the limestone of Hill Top as you drop downwards to a barn across a stile in a wall, to the lush wooded area of Twiston Bottoms. Here you will meet the stream which you must follow through cloisters of trees, and then across a flat rough pastured field to a small wicker gate. This leads across a footbridge onto the road. Continuing along the road for a couple of hundred yards will bring you to Twiston Mill.

A stile by a gate leads to the seclusion of a field and your path follows the beck on your left through a metal gate. Ahead two stiles line up your way to skirt the end of Torrid Bank Wood to a foot-bridge. Cross this and following the side of the wall make your way up to the farm on the skyline. Pass through the gate and straight through the yard turning the last building on your right. There is no stile but pass through the gate immediately in front of you, and through a second 50 yards ahead. Turn left and follow the fence up to a line of trees. The path follows this up and over the crest of the hill to a stile in a wall.

This is Wooly Hill and the highest part of the walk. Your path leads straight across the ridge with outstandingly good views in all directions. Continue on this route crossing numerous stiles until you approach the road on your left, and a fence stretches off to your right and Hey House Farm to the right of a copse of trees. Follow the fence on your right towards the farm to pick up the unmetalled road leading to it. Just in front of the farm is a gate in the wall through which you must go. Keep to the side of the field you have entered to pick up the old Roman Road which is followed at this point. Nothing remains to be seen of it here but the path leads in a typically straight line skirting the left of the buildings and the wood to cross two fields by way of stiles. In a third field a gate in a fence leads you past Hall Royds Wood, and from here the tower of Downham church can be clearly seen. If you look carefully at the contours in your immediate vicinity you should be able to pick out the flat area of the Roman road at this stage. Ahead, a quarter of a mile away, is a well wooded area for which you must make. The path leads to a wall which you should follow downwards to your left to emerge through a stile into the village of Downham and back to your car.

THE SABDEN-ROUGHLEE VALLEY

THIS valley, designated an area of natural beauty in which building is restricted, is a typical example of Pendleside scenery. It has a quiet dignified charm which contrasts sharply with the neighbouring industrial valley running parallel with it on the other side of the Noggarth ridge.

One of the most delightful walks I know begins at Sabden, and keeping mainly to the crest of the ridge, takes you all the length of the valley to Blacko. On your left the whole valley is laid out before you, whilst on your right the industrial towns of Burnley, Brierfield, and Nelson sprawl grotesquely, and are enclosed by the ring of Hambledon and Boulsworth. This is a walk where you can stride out for most of the way, the route unfolding clearly ahead. Unfortunately it is a full day's walk, and therefore cannot be included in this guide. I have therefore split it into four shorter walks using three bases situated at:

1. Higherford
2. Newchurch in Pendle
3. Sabden.

These walks, though lacking the atmosphere of freedom one gets when striding out unchallenged on a ridge, nevertheless give immense satisfaction from the variety and everchanging scenery. Indeed the whole area is criss-crossed by a warren of footpaths that demand further exploration.

Walk 2   The Water Meetings from Higherford

Grade—Easy.
Distance—approximately 3 miles.
Time—about 2 hours.

BEFORE the era of the motorcar, when families enjoyed simpler pleasures, the Watermeetings at Higherford was a favourite picnic spot. Here small children frolicked in the water or played with bat and ball on the grass, whilst courting couples shouldered their way along wooded secluded paths. Today few venture on these paths, and the merriment and laughter of the children has changed to the gentle burbble of the water and the song of the birds. This is now a peaceful walk, suitable for an evening stroll or a morning's exercise before lunch.

At Higherford Bridge where the main road crosses Pendle Water

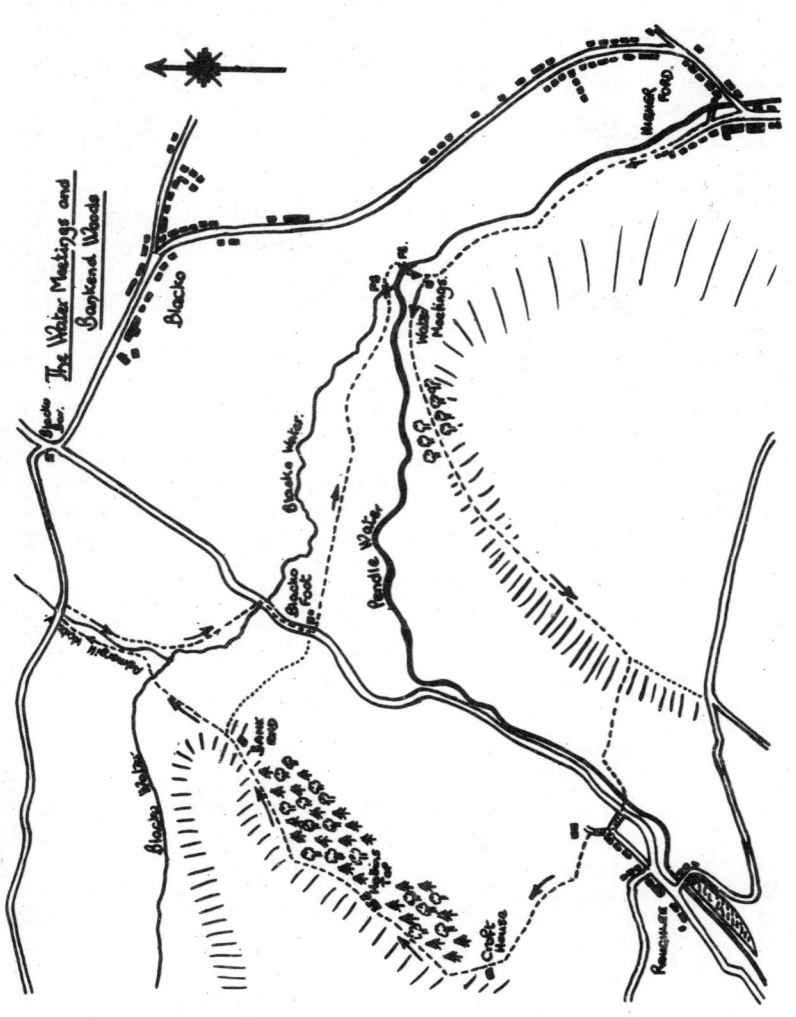

there is a narrow road following the lefthand bank of the river. Take this and you will find adequate space within 200 yards to park your car.

The route begins and ends here.

Walk to the end of the lane where you will find ready access to the fields by a narrow swing gate alongside the river bank. The path follows the river closely, passing Holme Tennis Club on your left and eventually arriving at the Water Meetings Farm.

A few years ago, Pendle Water became a seething torrent which flooded much of Barrowford downstream causing tremendous damage. A landslip action took away half of the main road, and the scars of that devastating flood may still be seen as you wander slowly upstream. Some attempt has been made to prevent a reoccurrence of this catastrophe by building stone walls at various points of erosion of the river bank. Stone grykes, or barriers, also cross the river's path in an effort to break up any surging water, and prevent the rolling of huge boulders downstream

At the Water Meetings Farm two paths become apparent. One crosses the bridge and this will be a part of the return route; whilst the other leads through a stile on your left. Take this latter route to the left hand bank of the river and follow a distinct path leading to a copse of mixed bushes and trees.

After crossing the stile, the path continues upwards becoming narrower as it seems to force a way between the numerous holly bushes. Occasional glimpses on the right reveal the stark outline of Wheathead, whilst Bank End woods clothe the slopes ahead. At a point where your lungs begin to protest, about half way though the wood, the path appears to fork. Take the upper path even though your way seems to be barred, and you will emerge from the trees within the next 100 yards.

Ahead a fence and stile yields access to more open ground with clear views to your right. The path follows a line of hawthorne trees and a wooded fence until it meets a stone wall. Here a stile besides a gate forces you over into an open field, though your route continues in the same direction along a ridge but on the other side of the wall. You can now stride out boldly crossing another stile in your path until eventually you meet a stile in the wall on your left hand.

A pause at this point to reflect on your route is advisable, since straight ahead the path leads first to the main road and then on to Ridgaling Reservoir. The stile cutting across your route represents another path leading you directly downwards towards Roughlee. There is no apparent path here so make your own way downwards at right angles to your original route. As the righthand edge of Roughlee village comes into view make your way directly for it and eventually you will see a series of concrete stepping stones crossing Pendle Water to the main road.

Across the road you must follow the direction of the footpath sign which says 'Croft House ¼ mile'. Directly ahead where the lane bends right is a metal gate through which you must pass. Follow the double cart track keeping the hedge on your left through another gate, to where the cart track becomes indistinct in about 100 yards. On your right is an obvious depression which is also the line of the footpath through the tall meadow grass terminating in a wooden stile. Crossing a second stile and a second field make your way to the right hand side of the buildings at Croft House Farm. Once round the buildings ignore the metal gate on your left and continue along the hedgeside and cross a stile in the corner of the field. A short steep climb terminates in a stile crossing to a bridle path and this leads on your right to Hollins.

Hollins Farm nestles into the wooded hillside and the path goes over a stile on the lefthand side of the building to emerge above Bank End Woods. Directly ahead is a barn which you must make for crossing a stile by a gate and then another stile on the left of the building. Immediately over this stile you are confronted by two gates and no apparent route. Make for the lefthand one and a stile just round the corner leads you on the right path. With Blacko Tower as your marker, you may now stride out across the fields parallel to the line of Bank End Woods, at the end of which a metal gate appears in a stone wall. Across the stile here, your path though indistinct makes downhill, still in the direction of Blacko Tower, to an open gateway at the bottom end of the field. In the next field your route follows closely the line of electricity poles until a clump of haw-thorne bushes are reached. Pass them on the right and make your way straight downwards to a stile over a fence and a small beck at the bottom of the hill. Once across the beck your route follows the lefthand bank of the main stream emerging at the road by the side of the bridge.

Turn right on the road and cross the bridge. Go over the stile and down the stone steps to the other side of the river known as Admergill Water. Follow the bank downstream until you again emerge onto the road leading from Roughlee to Blacko. Turn right here and walk up the road until you come to Blacko Foot Farm. A footpath sign directs you through the farm yard and a gate into a meadow. Follow the line of trees and fence on your left in a straight line for about ¼ mile. Your route will now begin to drop downwards towards the Water Meetings and ahead you will see a footbridge which you should make for. Once across this, continue along the river bank and turn right across the bridge to bring you back to the Water Meetings Farm.

The way back to your car now retraces your footsteps earlier on.

Walk 3   Newchurch and the Noggarth Ridge

Grade—Easy, shoes adequate except when wet.
Time—approximately 2 hours.
Distance—4-5 miles.

PROBABLY the most interesting story to be told of this district is that of the Pendle Witches. Newchurch in Pendle is right at the heart of this seventeenth century melodrama, and the grave of Richard Nutter and his wife Margaret is to be seen just to the right of the main entrance to the church. Richard was the brother-in-law of Dame Alice Nutter of Roughlee, who along with Old Mother Demdike and others were committed as witches to Lancaster Castle and there executed.

Newchurch in Pendle nestles into the hillside known as Goldshaw Booth and it is the base for the second walk in the series covering the Sabden-Roughlee valley. The only convenient parking is the private car park belonging to the Lamb Inn. However, this is rarely full and permission to park is readily obtained.

Leaving the car park turn downhill on the road that leads to Roughlee, and on the opposite side almost directly in front of you, is a stile which is the start to your journey. Once in the field you will perceive ahead a wall which acts as a boundary to an afforested conifer belt of trees. Two stiles may be seen, the lower one on the right hand side of a line of electricity poles, and the upper one, the one you must make for, more on the skyline. Cross the upper stile in the wall and a second wooden one and follow the distinct track leading through the conifers. Half way through the wood a wall with another stone stile must be crossed, and a further stile on emerging from the trees.

You are now in a very rough pasture on the crest almost of a ridge. Ahead a group of trees directs your path. As you approach them you will be aware that the track converges with a wall on your left. Follow this wall which acts as a boundary to a second wooded conifer belt, and with the beacon of Blacko Tower directly ahead continue until you are confronted by a wall and the end of the trees on your left. Here a stile with a wooden swing gate allows you access to another field, and the track though now indistinct follows the wall on your right down the hill.

A stile at the end of this field opens on to an old grassy lane. This was the old road linking Barley with Thorneyholme and Roughlee.

Newchurch and the Noggarth Ridge.

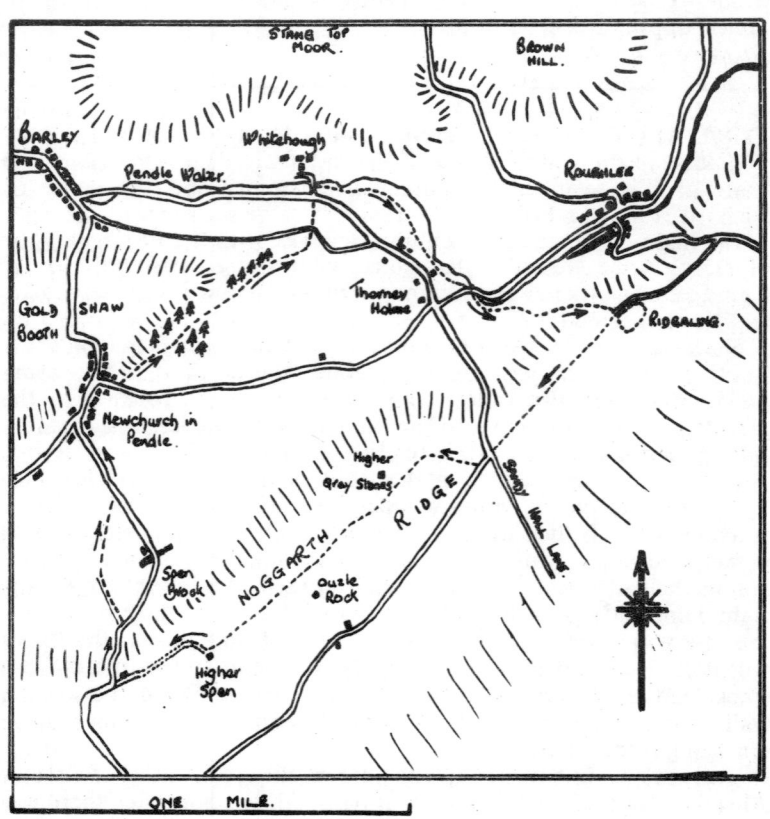

Cross the lane, and go through the narrow stile at the other side and make your way directly down the hill to emerge at the main road via at gate.

Across the main road a cobbled lane dips downwards to White hough. It is well signposted by a sign on the left reading Whitehough Camp School and on the right a footpath sign. Go down this lane to the bridge at the bottom crossing Pendle Water. On the right just in front of the bridge is a gate and stile, which leads you downstream towards some tall trees. A stone stile leads into a field in which the river has meandered during the course of its history leaving evidence of its various channels by its legacy of levees. Make for the distinctive farmhouse at Thorneyholme and as you pass through the stile by the water's edge you will see a small metal swing gate ahead. Take the path through this gate which is narrowed by a wall on your right and the bank of Pendle Water on your left until you arrive at the main road by an iron bridge.

Directly across the road a footpath sign reads Ridgaling ¾ mile. Take this path which again leads you along the river bank for about 100 yards, then past a line of hawthorne bushes. Here the track begins to strike upwards through an extremely boggy morass to a fence, not clearly evident at first, with a wooden stile in it. Pick your way once across the stile to a tall tree on your left on the skyline. On arrival follow the wall uphill until you find a stone stile on your left after about 50 yards. Across this the path takes a direct line to two other stiles eventually skirting above a caravan site and then aiming for a sturdy wall which is the boundary of Ridgaling Reservoir. This latter section of the walk affords quite extraordinary views of Blacko Tower slightly to your left, and Bank End Woods across on the other side of the valley. Once the wall comes in view make for a small stone built pump house at the right where you will find a stile crossing into the lane.

Turn right in the lane, and with the wall and then a fence and hedge on your right, follow the cart-track. After about quarter of a mile an open gateway allows you access into another field, where you now follow close by a wall on your left to emerge at the main road at the top of Sandy Hall Lane.

Across the stile walk straight ahead along the road until you come to the first footpath sign on your right which reads 'Lower Gray Stones, Dimpenley ¾ mile. Go through the stile and make your way diagonally across the field to the end of a wall on your left. Do not go through the gate in the wall but turn the end of it and make for a gate directly ahead by a line of hawthornes.

This gate allows you acces to an unmetalled road linking Higher Gray Stones Farm with the main road. Go across it and straight ahead a stile will be seen in a stone wall. Make for this across open pasture and having crossed, the stile, follow the wall on your right in a direct line with the T.V. aerial which stands out like a sore finger ahead. At this point the path completely disappears but this beacon is better than any signpost so cross the open rough pasture along what is now the Noggarth Ridge. Somewhere along this route you will cross another path which links Higher Gray Stones Farm with Ouzel Rock Farm ignore this and continue on in the same direction as before. Eventually you will see a stile leading to a path between a hedge on your right and a barbed fence close on your left. Continue along over three stiles and passing a farm on your left hand. The vista before you yields a panoramic view of the Sabden Valley, with Newchurch entrenched on the sides of Goldshaw Booth and backed by the brooding shape of Pendle.

Make your way to the left hand corner of the field, through a stile and then make for the right hand end of a wall crossing your path at right angles. Here you will pick up a cart-track linking High Spen Farm with the main road, and which you should follow past a water-logged quarry on your right and emerge at the main road by the side of a picturesque cottage.

Turn right and go down the road for about 300 yards until you see a footpath sign which reads Newchurch $\frac{1}{2}$ mile. The way is now quite evident crossing two fields to meet the main road again which you then must follow back to the village and your car.

Walk 4   The Sabden Valley

Grade—Easy—shoes quite adequate.
Time—2½ to 3 hours.
Distance—about 8 miles.

SABDEN is a sprawling village at the foot of the road leading over the Nick of Pendle to Clitheroe. It is rather remote and cut off from the industrial towns of Padiham and Burnley by the ridge called Padiham Heights, and by Black Hill. This ridge presents an escarpment in a WSW-ENE direction and the line of the footpath hugs close to this escarpment for the first part of the walk.

As you enter Sabden from the Padiham side a car park is signposted on your left, but I have always found room to leave my car on some spare ground next to a prominent chapel on your right opposite the road junction at the centre of the village. Leaving your car here is convenient as the continuation of the unmetalled lane is the start of the walk.

A hundred yards or so along this rough road cross Stubbins Lane and proceed on the left of some Old Folks Bungalows at Little Moor Close. A well defined unmetalled bridle path now stretches out for approximately a mile.

The Sabden valley stretches before you, ringed on the right by the escarpment of Padiham Heights and on the left by the gentler slopes leading upwards to Spence Moor, an outlying moorland tongue of Pendle. The valley is flat, the going is easy and there is plenty of time to gaze around.

Just beyond a small clump of trees, the first you have seen on this path, is Dean; an old farmstead with stone mullioned windows and an inscription above that wind and weather have eroded and almost obliterated. Here the footpath diverges, one following the valley bottom goes to the left; and the other, the one you should take, crosses the bridge over Sabden Brook.

Follow the wallside on your left through a gate, and continue until the wall ends. A path strikes out here diagonally up the escarpment but ignore this and turn the end of the wall on your left. Here a well built stile takes you into the field alongside which you have been walking. Follow the wallside on your right that leads in the same direction as the escarpment. Go through a stile, and make your way to the right hand side of some buildings. This is Stone Edge Farm but is more quaintly referred to on Ordnance Survey Maps as "Back O' Th' Hill".

21

The Sabden Valley.

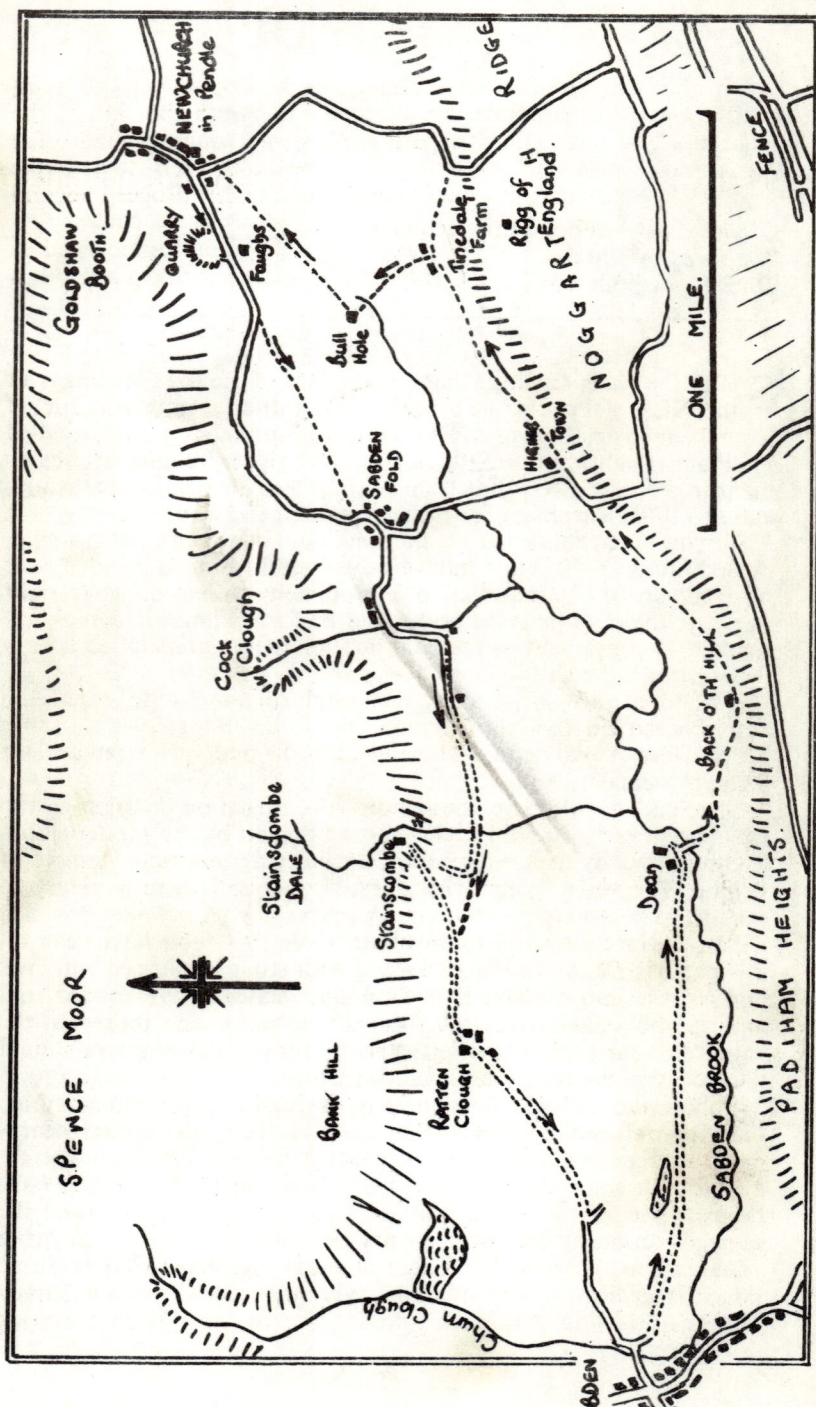

SPENCE MOOR

GOLDSHAW Booth.

NEWCHURCH in Pendle

QUARRY

Faughs

Bull Hole

SABDEN FOLD

Tindale Farm

Rigg of H

Cock Clough

Stainscombe Dale

Stainscombe

Bank Hill

Ratten Clough

Churn Clough

Back o' th' Hill

Dean

SABDEN BROOK.

PADIHAM HEIGHTS.

SABDEN

FENCE

RIDGE

NOGGARTENGLAND

Higham Town

ONE MILE.

Go over the stile besides the gate, ignore the unmetalled road leading up the escarpment, and keep parallel with the side of the buildings. The now indistinct path crosses very rough ground often oozing with water and squelching miserably with every step. Make for a gate ahead and following the wall on your left proceed beyond it to a stile. Once over the stile the path vanishes, but a chimney on the skyline is a good marker and you can stride out unmolested as this is a right of way finally leading over a cattle grid to a bend in the road to Sabden Fold.

Turn left along the road, directly ahead is Higher Town Farm about 150 yards away. Take the lane leading from the road and pass the back of the buildings on your left. Go through a gate and then follow the wallside. Newchurch, about 1½ miles distant, clings to the side of Goldshaw Booth, and the chimney of Spen Brook Mill lies directly ahead backed by Blacko Tower in the distance.

Cross the stile at the end of the pasture into a meadow, and make your way along the fence-side towards a solitary hawthorne tree about 100 yards ahead. A wall begins here stretching out towards Tynedale Farm which can be seen surrounded by trees ahead. Cross the stile by the wall and follow it to the farm buildings and a cobbled lane. Immediately past the farm buildings is a cottage and between the two a lane cuts down to your left leading to the Bull Hole Farm at the watershed of the valley. Ahead and to your right on the slopes of Goldshaw Booth you will see Faugh's Quarry which is the aim of this part of the walk.

Cross the stile at the end of the lane just before the Bull Hole and turning right follow the wallside towards a derelict building known as Moss End in a patch of trees. Just before you arrive there cross a stile so that you are on the other side of the wall, and still following it go alongside the back of Moss End. Make for an open gateway, across a field below Faugh's Farm, and go through an iron gate and over a stile opposite. The path now leads straight ahead over another stile to emerge on to the road just before it enters Newchurch and opposite the village school.

Turn left and then left again along the road signposted "Sabden Fold 1¼" and continue along this metalled road until, you reach the entrance to Faugh's Quarry on your right. This quarry contains the effigy of a man who was killed around the turn of the century, and his workmates carved his face in the rock in a lasting memory to him. It is, however, difficult to find. Go into the quarry and stand right in the centre so that you are surrounded on three sides by rock. Turn slowly on this spot using a compass until you are facing a magnetic bearing of 140 degrees. The face is at head height from the quarry floor and is now staring back at you.

Retrace your steps to the road, turn right and make your way for about 200 yards to where a footpath sign besides a stile reads "Sabden Fold ¾". Take this path leading to Well Head Cottage which is in front of you, and on passing it make your way to a stile leading down some steps into a dell besides a brook. Follow the brook downstream on its right, disregarding a path which leads upwards into the field, and make for the stile ahead. Once across this, the path follows the fence on your right and passes first a farm on your righthand and then another on your lefthand to emerge on to a cart track leading towards Cappers Farm. Before arriving at Cappers make for a stile which is to the left of the buildings and which takes you through a field alongside a line of electricity poles to the road leading into Sabden Fold.

Turn left, and as you come into Sabden Fold take the road leading right and signposted "Sabden. No through road. 2½ miles." For about ¾ mile your route follows the metalled surface of the road passing Cock Clough and finally Lower Lane Farm where it peters out into a greasy unmetalled lane. Continue along, passing a derelict building on your left and crossing a brook which has decended down the clough known as Stainscombe Dale. As the cart track climbs beyond the gate and turns to the right making up-wards for Stainscombe, continue in a straight line following closely the line of the fence and hedge on your left. As you top the crest of the rise a barn comes into view, make for the righthand side of it where you will pick up the cart track once more. This now leads directly to Ratten Clough Farm and here a path strikes out to the right of the buildings along the wallside for Churn Clough. Do not take this however, as your route goes through the farm yard between the buildings and emerges on a double concrete roadway which takes you all the way down into Sabden about 1 mile distant.

GERRARD PUBLICATIONS

From BOOKSELLERS or GERRARD Publications
6, Edge End Avenue, Brierfield, Nelson, Lancs.
Telephone: Nelson (0282)-63321

TWIXT THEE AND ME
An anthology of Yorkshire and Lancashire verse and prose, selected and edited by Joan Pomfret · 232pp.

			postage
0 900397 26 8	limp	£1.35	13p
0 900397 25 X	hardback	£2.50	16p

LANCASHIRE EVERGREENS
A hundred old favourite poems
selected and edited by Joan Pomfret.
2nd edition 1973, 196 pp.

0 900397 02 0	limp	£1.00	11p

PENNINE PANORAMA by Peter Wightman
People and places, past and present
in and around the Central Pennines
15 full page drawings, 196 pp. M8, 1968

0 900 397 15 2	cloth	£1.75	16p

THE LANCASHIRE WITCHES by Harrison Ainsworth
The most famous of northern classics 572 pp.
0 090 397 0 71 3rd impression 1972

	cloth	95p	11p

BOOKS FOR WALKERS

NEW 1974

PENDLESIDE AND BRONTE COUNTRY
WALKS FOR MOTORISTS by George Banks
30 circular walks, 30 sketch maps, photographs

0 900397 28 4		55p

NORTH YORK MOORS WALKS FOR MOTORISTS.
NORTH AND EAST by Geoffrey White
30 circular walks, 30 sketch maps, illustrations

0 900397 29 2		55p

PREVIOUSLY PUBLISHED
NORTH YORK MOORS WALKS FOR MOTORISTS
WEST and SOUTH by Geoffrey White.
30 circular walks, maps and illustrations.
0 900 397 24 1   50p

LAKE DISTRICT WALKS FOR MOTORISTS by John Parker

Central Area · Grasmere, Ambleside,
Windermere, Coniston.
0 900 397 06 3   3rd Impression 1973   55p

Northern Area · Keswick, Borrowdale, Ullswater
0 900 397 19 5 3rd Impression 1974 (with revisions)
                                                  55p

Western Area · Buttermere, Wastwater, Eskdale,
Duddon Valley, West of Coniston and to the coast
0 900 397 23 3   1973   55p

Each of the three volumes describes 30 circular walks
from the car back to the car (parking location given)
and contains 30 sketch maps and illustrations.

PEAK DISTRICT WALKS FOR MOTORISTS by C. Thompson
30 circular walks, with maps and illustrations.
0 900 397 20 9   1972   50p

Ramblers Association titles

WALKS FOR MOTORISTS IN THE YORKSHIRE DALES
30 circular walks.
0 900 397 13 45   8th Impression 1974   55p

FURTHER DALES WALKS FOR MOTORISTS
30 circular walks.
0 900 397 05 5   4th Impression 1973   50p

THE DALES WAY   50p
A continuous footpath from Ilkley in
Wharfedale to Bowness on Windermere
0 900 397 04 7   3rd impression 1972   42½p
Sketch maps in every volume

WALKING THE PENNINE WAY by A. P. Binns
with maps and illustrations.
0 900 397 21 7   2nd revised edition 1972   50p

WALKS IN HODDER COUNTRY
by Alan Lawson who also drew the sketch maps
W00 417 41   22½p

Postages: add 7p for one book,
plus 6p for every additional book

Walk 5

Churn Clough and the Whins from Sabden

Grade—Easy.
Distance.—3-4 miles.
Time—about 2 hours.

FOR some reason unknown to myself Sabden has always been the butt of local humour. As a child I was brought up to believe that the main industry in the village was Treacle Mining, and that it was inhabited by hobgoblins. Perhaps in some way I may be responsible for perpetuating this sort of legend, for when my daughter was small I set off one morning and 'Salted' a particular hawthorne tree in Churn Clough. Later in the day I ambled along with a small band of children to take them on the walk described here, and to encourage their weary legs I told them a story as we went along about a Lollipop tree; the only one in existence which was supposed to grow somewhere around Sabden. Of course you can imagine the shrieks of delight and the expressions on their little faces when the tree in question was discovered. The illusion however, was completely shattered when one older and more sophisticated child exclaimed "but I'm sure they don't grow with cellophane paper wrapped around them."

The reason for this tale is to emphasise that this walk is suitable for a young family since there is little climbing and the distance involved is short. For very young children however I cannot promise the tree will be bearing fruit.

Park your car on the spare ground at the side of the Methodist Chapel in Sabden, which is opposite the T junction in the centre of the village. Go around the front of the chapel to Wesley Street for this is where the walk begins.

At the end of Wesley Street is St. Nicholas' Church; indeed for the size of the population, Sabden seems to be very well endowed with spiritual guidance. Follow the road around to the left, and in about 200 yards you will find it diverging to the right as a metalled roadway leading up to Ratten Clough; and to the left as an unfinished rough surface crossing a small bridge. Take the latter route across the bridge and follow its winding path upwards until a line of houses confronts you. Make your way to the left hand side of this row where a wooden wicker gate takes you into a field.

The path, not very evident, strikes out along the fence on your right, and as you gain height over a slight incline you will see the

Churn Clough and The Whins from Sabden

Bank Hill
Ratten Clough Farm
Sabden Brook
Calf Hill
Sabden
Nick of Pendle
Parsley Barn
Higher Whins
Whins House
Wiswell Moor
Willan Hays Farm
Wiswell Moor House

next stile in the corner of the field. Through this stile the path goes up a long narrow field boarded on one side by a fence and on the other by Churn Clough Beck. Ahead and slightly right of where you are heading is Calf Hill, and on your right a coppice of deciduous trees hides the reservoir behind Churn Clough. Go through the gate at the top of the field to follow the left hand bank of a tributary stream of Churn Clough Beck. Pass through another gate and over a stile to emerge on to the open hillside. Make your way still upwards until you pick up a distinct unmetalled roadway running across your path from left to right. Turn left and follow it towards the main road which leads over the Nick of Pendle.

Once you arrive at the main road turn uphill and walk about 200 yards to where a footpath sign proclaims a Bridlepath and route to Wisewell 2$\frac{1}{4}$ miles and Whalley 3$\frac{1}{4}$ miles on your left. Go through the gate and follow the path down to Parsley Barn. On the far side of the barn a footpath leads across the fields directly to some trees above Higher Whins, and this can be taken if you wish to shorten the walk. If not, proceed onwards passing Wilkin Heys Farm and on to Wisewell Moor Farm about 1$\frac{1}{4}$ miles from the footpath sign.

From here the path cuts diagonally back across the open field to a gateway in the fence about $\frac{1}{4}$ mile distant to the right of a copse of trees. On passing through the gateway the track turns left along the bottom side of the trees and down the hill to cross an open clough at the bottom where the slope flattens out.

Through a wicker gate the path now makes for the lefthand side of some tall deciduous trees and as you approach you will see an iron swing gate close alongside them. Continuing in the same direction following a fence on your right brings you to the farm buildings of Higher Whins. Go over a stile to the right, skirting the top side of Whins House. On your left are three small out buildings near to a gate and sturdy stile. Go over the stile and follow the line of the fence on your right eventually to arrive at the road going up the Nick of Pendle. Turn right and retrace your steps to your car.

Walk 6   Whalley Nab and Read Hall

Distance—about 7 to 8 miles.
Grade—Moderate-easy going suitable for strong shoes.
Time—allow about 2½ to 3 hours for walking.

WHALLEY is situated at the southernmost flanks of Pendle where its gradiants gradually ease into the valley bottom in which the River Calder meanders gently on a westerly course. It is a historic town, where the remains of a Benedictine Abbey are well worth a visit. To the east lies Read Hall where Roger Nowell, a Justice of the Peace, resided during the turbelent times of the Pendle witches. The district steeped in history is never the less one of scenic beauty, charm and ever changing views, and the walk described is probably best walked in full summer to fully appreciate them.

Leaving the car park in the very centre of Whalley, turn left along the Preston road and cross the bridge over the River Calder. The main road here takes a sharp right hand bend, but in the corner a narrow road winds steeply up the flanks of Whalley Nab. Follow this incline for about 100 yards, until a paved lane strikes out to your left. This lane is walled on your left hand and passes through a well wooded slope as it rapidly carries you upwards. Below and to your left Whalley and the Calder are spread out for your inspection, whilst the lane soon gives way to a brief earthy track following a fence. Eventually the gradiant begins to ease, and though the summit of the Nab is still above you on your right, the path flattens out and follows the contours of the hill to meet an unmelted roadway.

This leads to Procter's Farm and after about quarter of a mile to Whalley Banks Farm. Here a footpath sign reads 'Great Harwood', and points your way gently down a lane on your left.

The path now leaves all form of habitation behind, and begins to drop down through a wooded glade. A wooden swing gate at the end of the glade allows access to a field, and with Altham Gas Works cooling towers directly ahead sticking out like a sore thumb against the background of Hambledon, make your way straight down to a fence and a drainage ditch. Keep a careful lookout for a second swing gate taking you to the other side of the fence, and keeping still in the same direction a third swing gate soon appears.

About 50 yards beyond the last swing gate cross the stream in the corner of the field and pass between some hawthorne trees. Your path now makes directly towards two tall willow trees and from

28

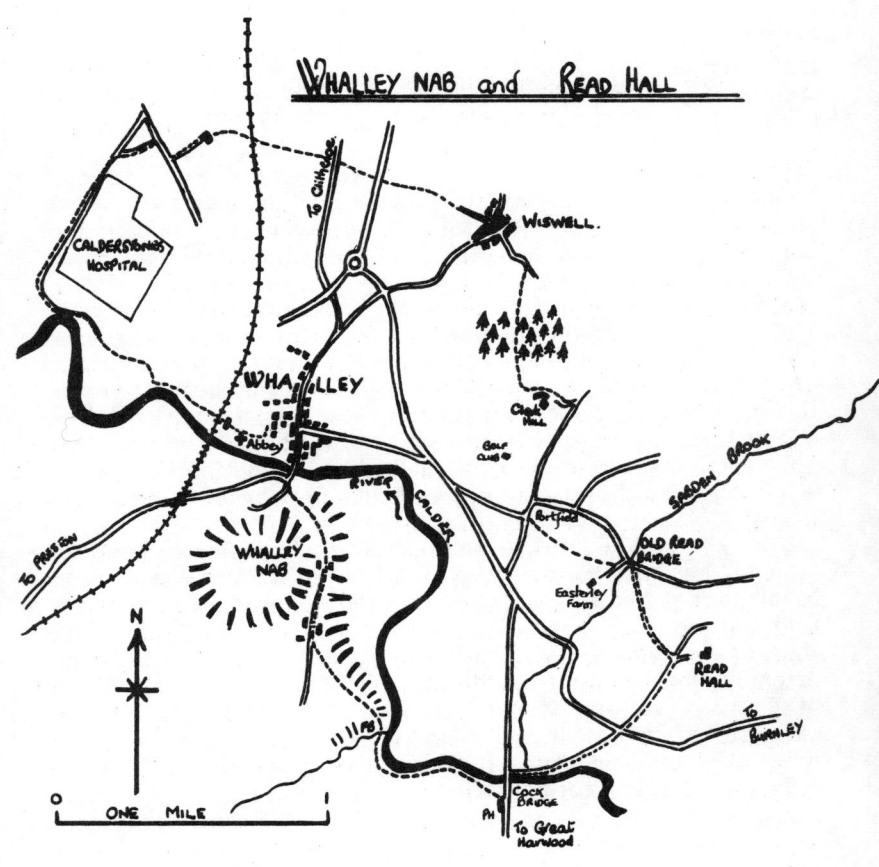

WHALLEY NAB and READ HALL

CALDERSTONES HOSPITAL

To Clitheroe

WISWELL.

WHALLEY

Abbey

Clerk Hill

GOLF CLUB

RIVER CALDER

SABDEN BROOK

To Preston

WHALLEY NAB

Portfield

OLD READ BRIDGE

Easterley Farm

READ HALL

To Burnley

N

O   ONE   MILE   I

PH

Cock Bridge

To Great Harwood

there downwards to cross a small tributary stream by means of a stone footbridge.

The path now ascends, first over a stile, and then by a short but sharp climb in a well wooded section. Where it levels out follow the path ignoring a stile on your right and make for one directly ahead. Once over this stile two paths diverge, the right hand one follows the fence line, whilst the lefthand one keeps close to a line of trees on the very edge of a steep descent into the Calder. Follow the latter path dropping downwards to cross another tributary stream and then wend your way along the river bank until eventually the path brings you out on to the main Accrington Road at the 'Game Cock Inn.'

Cross the road and turning left make your way over Cock Bridge to the first opening on your right marked with a large sign "Read Nurseries". Follow the metalled roadway until you are near the Nursery and then take the grassy lane which leads you right up to the main Whalley-Burnley road.

Straight across the main road is the grand entrance to Read Hall. Though not marked, this driveway is a public right of way and takes you through pleasant parkland towards Read Hall. About a quarter of a mile from the main road, where the driveway swings right towards the Hall, and an unmetalled roadway continues through a broad belt of trees, a five barred gate and stile will be seen on your left. This gives access to a footpath which skirts the bottom end of the woods, closely following it, to emerge on a minor road by Read Old Bridge.

Turn left, cross the bridge and take the first opening on your left marked "Easterley Farm." On your right hand at the first slight bend in this farm path a stile takes you by a right of way directly to Port-field and the road. You now have the choice of cutting your walk short by following the road back into Whalley about 1 mile distant, or continuing by turning right and following the road signposted "Cul de Sac" for approximately ½ mile to Clerk Hill. Pass the main entrance to Clerk Hill and CONTINUE until you come to an unmetalled road on your left which leads round the back of the estate to Clerk Hill cottages. Go along this road for 50 yards or so and then through a gate on your right to follow a distinct bridle path as it curves round to the left. Eventually it meets a fence and gate. Go through the gate and follow the fence which turns you gradually right until you come to an afforested belt of conifers.

Where the bridle path meets the conifers go through the gate and then immediately turn and go over the stile to enter a cloistered pathway which takes you through the wood after about ¼ mile. You will emerge from the wood over a stile and into a field; direct your steps across the field and then downwards to meet a road called Moor Lane. Follow this lane downwards into Wiswell village.

Straight across the T junction of Moor Lane with the main road passing through Wiswell is a narrow lane called Vicarage Fold which will take you past "The Freemasons Arms" to a road leading to Barrow. Straight across this road and slightly to your left is the entrance of Vicarage Farm by way of a cattle grid and concrete drive. Make your way up this drive and to a gate in the corner of the yard. This leads you into a wide grassy roadway which eventually peters out after about 200 yards. Make for a gateway directly ahead and once through this turn right and cross to a concealed stile in the corner of the field. Turn left over this stile and follow the hedgerow on your left down to the new and very busy Whalley/Clitheroe road. Cross over carefully and go over the stile on the opposite banking to follow the hedgerow on your right through two other stiles to eventually emerge on the main Barrow road.

Directly opposite a stile takes you into a field and the path though not distinct follows the fence on your left. The end of the field is not marked by either a wall or fence so look carefully for the next stile on your left. This takes you over to the other side of the fence which you must still follow towards the railway ahead. Though no path is apparent you will come upon one as soon as you enter the trees ahead and this makes for a crossing of the railway track.

On the opposite side of the railway go through a gate and follow the hedge until you come to a small stile and footbridge over a stream. Directly ahead another stile in a fence points the way you have to take, and on reaching this a second stile besides some buildings comes into view. Go through the swing gate here and over another small footbridge and then turn right following the stream to emerge on an unmetalled farm yard at Brook House. This lane will now take you down to the main road ahead.

Turn right on the road and then left again at the telephone kiosk to go along a Cul-de-Sac called Kingsmill Avenue. At the end of this avenue a stile and stoney track leads you to a lane in about 50 yards. Turn left along this lane and follow it for approximately 1 mile around the back of Calderstones Hospital. Where the lane ends cross a stile and continue to follow the railings on your lefthand side. These leads you to a second lane and when this terminates a well made stile will be seen ahead. However instead of making for it diverge to the right and head by a narrow path to the river side. Follow the river bank until you are abreast of the Sewrage Works where you can turn left into a grassy lane. Follow this lane which leads you under the New Road and then emerges at a road by the Railway Viaduct. Go under the viaduct and beneath the Abbey Gateway to enter Whalley. From here make your way to the centre and back to your car.

Walk 7　　　　Mearley Moor from Pendleton

Grade—Moderate. Boots strongly recommended as there is some
　　rough ground to cover.
Distance—about 6 miles.
Time—allow 3-3½ hours (though this does not allow for stops.)

BY comparison with Donwham, Penldeton is a quiet little village;
　　yet in my opinion is it the prettiest in the surrounding area. It
has two unique features. Firstly, the Public House in the main street
rejoices in the unusual name of "The Swan with Two Necks", and
if you retire there for liquid refreshment after you walk I am sure
you will hear an entertaining yarn from the Landlord on its origin.
Secondly, the main street of the village is neatly bisected by Swardean
Brook which carouses gaily between two rows of sombre gritstone
dwellings facing each other like armies before a battle.

Parking in the village should promote no problem, so leaving your
car somewhere convenient make your way to the top lefthand end
of the village where the road leaves towards Worston. Just before
you arrive at the village school on your left, you will see two footpath
signs on your right besides a grassy lane. The first reads "Wiswell
1¾ miles", the second "Nick of Pendle 1¼ miles".

Go up the lane which follows the side of Swardean Beck until it
turns a sharp left. Ahead of you a gate and stile pass into a field and
follow the brook for about ¼ mile before arriving at a wooden footbridge. Cross over the stream and climb diagonally up to a tall tree
and a hedge on your left. Now follow the hedgeline up the slope in the
direction of the Well Springs public house which can just be seen
from here. Ahead a line of hawthorne trees cross your path; but pass
through them and make to a second such hedge of hawthornes
where you will find a gate in the hedge on your right. The footpath
goes through here and crosses the top of the field to an open gateway.
Turn left here and follow the hedge on your left up the slope until
the buildings of Wymondhouses come into view and a stile is seen
in a wall on the left of the buildings.

Crossing the stile brings you out onto open rough pasture. Go to
the left of the house and make your way towards an obvious track
which climbs diagonally upwards from right to left. Follow this track
which runs parallel to a stone wall about 50 yards distant and at a
higher level, and when you see an open gateway make for it. Go
through this and then crossing the contours more rapidly, ascend

Mearley Moor from Pendleton.

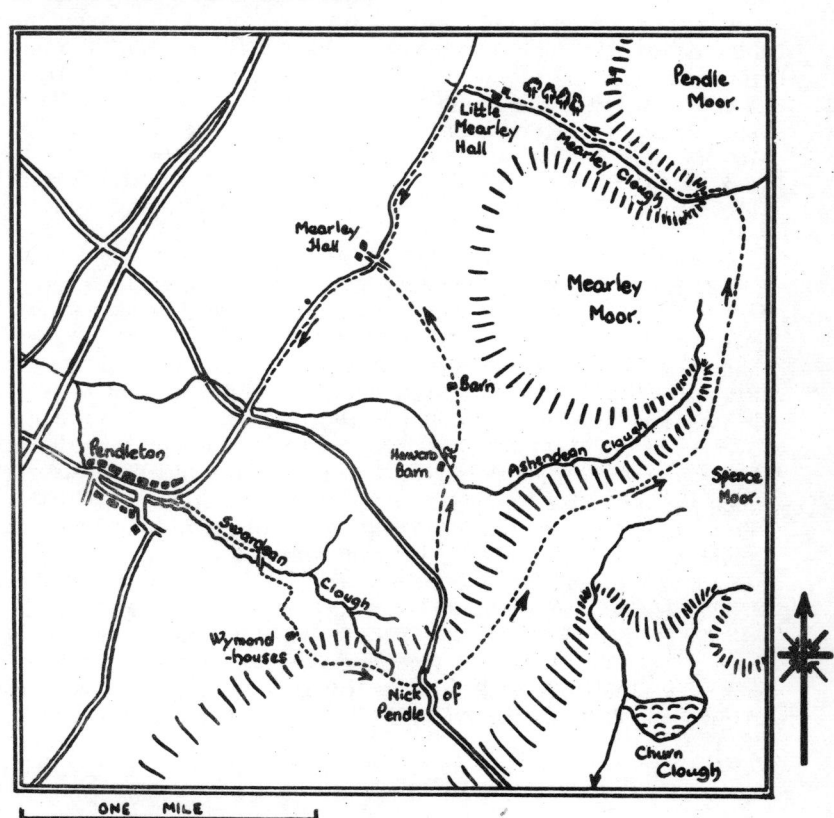

Pendle Moor.

Little Mearley Hall

Mearley Clough

Mearley Hall

Mearley Moor.

Barn

Ashendean Clough

Howcro Barn

Spence Moor.

Pendleton

Swardean Clough

Wymond -houses

Nick of Pendle

Churn Clough

ONE MILE

with the wall on your left until you meet a well made wooden stile mounting a stone wall across your path. Once across the stile your way becomes obvious and makes directly for the Nick of Pendle, emerging on to the open road by a gate.

On your right the road drops away to Sabden in a steep descent, whilst on your left it descends, though not as steeply, to the Wellsprings Hotel. No doubt you will want to rest for a few moments after the last section of the climb, so while you are doing so, comtemplate the map on the previous page. Two routes are open to you, a short one involving the descent to the Wellsprings and from there striking out across the shoulder of the moor to Howcroft's Barn, then by way of a second barn on the skyline, to drop downwards to Mearley Hall. The second route, the more tortuous one, follows the track along the ridge from the Nick of Pendle up towards Spence Moor and Mearley Moor which constitute the outlying arms of Pendle itself.

For just over a mile the track from the Nick wends its way, slowly gaining height, until it flattens out on Spence Moor at about 1,450 ft. At this point you must strike out directly Northwards straight across the open moor with no footpath to follow; for approximately a mile, that is about 20 minutes of hard rough walking. No doubt the distance will be measured more accurately by the amount of perspiration lost and muttered words about the author. Eventually, however, you will stand at the top of Mearley Clough, and after a short pause you should descend on the right hand side of the stream which cascades and tumbles quickly across the contours. Cross a stile in a wall at the bottom, 50 yards to the right of where the stream goes through the wall, and follow a wall on your right down into a wooded dell. From these trees you will emerge at Little Mearley Hall. Go through the farm yard and down the lane to meet a broad unmetalled roadway. Turn left and follow it, eventually passing Mearley Hall, and emerging onto the main Clitheroe—Nick of Pendle road via Pendleton House. Go across the road and take the metalled by-road which leads back to Pendleton in ½ mile.

Walk 8   Pendle Hill from Worston

Grade—Strenuous. Boots should be worn for this walk.
Time—allow between 3 and 4 hours
Distance—about 6 miles.

PENDLE, a majestic monarch in the surrounding landscape, commands a lingering respect from what ever viewpoint it is seen. Formed of alternating bands of sandstone and shales which dip gradually southeastwards, it has an underlying base of Carboniferous limestone which peeps out on its north and west edges. Capping the top is a hard band of Millstone Grit, known as Pendle Top Grit, which has successfully resisted weathering. The hill is therefore known geologically as an OUTLIER, that is, its summit is composed of young rock completely surrounded by older rock. Other hills typical of this formation can easily be seen from its summit; Ingleborough, Whernside, Penyghent, to name but a few.

Of the many pilgrimages I have made to its summit none is more exhilarating and satisfying as the conquest of Mearley Clough. It is as steep as the Lakeland fells, demanding concentration and will power to force each tired step, and yet its upper reaches give a delightful scramble if you keep to the bed of the stream. In winter festooned with icicles and clothed in snow it takes on the mantle of an Alpine climb as you kick steps in order to gain height.

Worston is the base from which to set out on this venture. It is a sleepy little village neglected by the modern by-pass linking Clitheroe with Guisburn over the hill. Here you may have to use the private car park belonging to the Calf's Head, or if you continue along the road to Downham as you pass out of the village via a double bend you will find space on the grass verge to park your car.

On the last bend as you leave Worston for Downham, where the road curves left, a large house will be seen set back from the road and connected to it by a gravel driveway across a small bridge. The walk begins here. Go across the bridge and immediately turn right and go between some farm buildings to a gate and stile directly ahead. Once through the stile the path follows the wall on the left, and when this ends, it makes for a tall solitary tree in the middle of the field. Beyond is a wooden stile which leads still in the same direction to a second field. Beyond this the path follows a wire fence on its right until it merges with a cart track coming in from the left. Turn right on

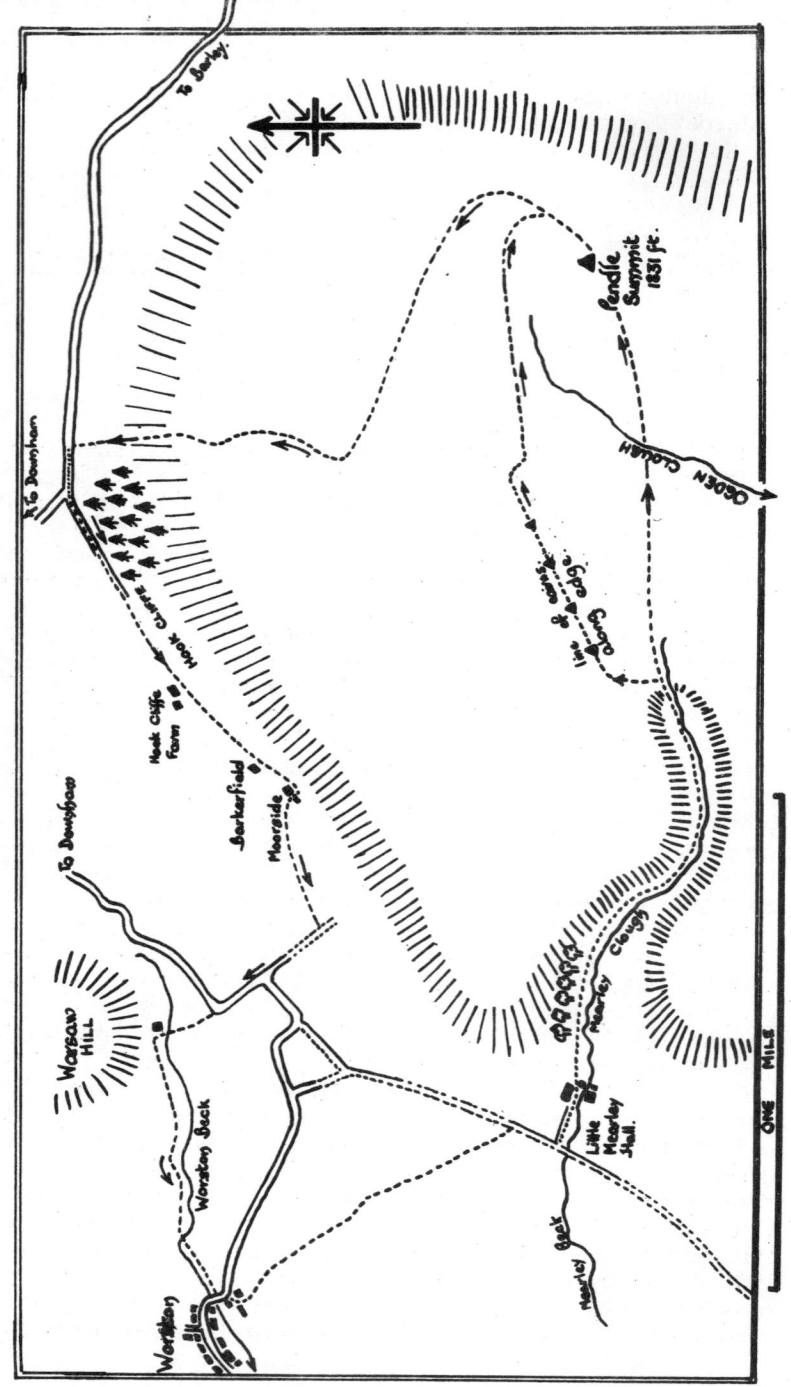

To Barley.

Pendle Summit 1831 ft.

OGDEN CLOUGH

To Downham

Wood Clough

Nook Cliffs Farm

Line of ridge

from below

Barkerfield

Moorside

Mearley Clough

To Downham

Little Mearley Hall.

Mearley Beck

Worsaw Hill

Worstons Back

Worston

Beadles

ONE MILE

this double track and in a few yards the lane linking it with Little Mearley Hall takes you up towards Pendle.

So far the countryside has had a lush green appearance due no doubt to the mixed underlying Yoredale rocks. Now the vegetation changes as you pass through Little Mearley Farm, for after a pleasant coppice, you emerge onto the acid peaty soil so typical of gritstone country.

To my knowledge, for twenty years, the farmer at Little Mearley has always had a noisy pack of dogs. Fortunately they are always chained, or going through the farmyard might have resulted in a very hurried retreat. Go through the gate at the top of the farmyard and make for a second gate ahead leading into a well wooded clough down the centre of which Mearley Beck cascades and tumbles on its way to join the Ribble. The path now is quite clear and leads upwards through the trees. Now is the time to shorten your stride for soon you will have to. Eventually, emerging from the trees, the track follows a wall on the left on an ever steepening gradient, until it reaches an awkward stile in the corner of the field. I have found this stile so difficult that I have frequently dropped to the Beck below and crossed easily by the fence.

Ahead, the tumbling beck, docile in the summer sunshine, has during history sliced the hillside like a razor blade creating a scar which now commands your attention. Two courses are now open to you. You may either climb up the hillside keeping the beck on your right, or more daringly, keep to the bed of the stream. The latter is more interesting if you are well shod and if the stream is not in spate, and it becomes a satisfying scramble the higher you go.

At last after much loss of body perspiration and frequent stops to admire the view, the crest of Pendle will be reached. Here you can strike out directly across the peat hags on a compass bearing of 073 degrees magnetic, which course will bring you eventually to the summit cairn; or you can follow the line of cairns on the lefthand edge of the hill. The former course is for those who wish to impress their girl friends, for the walking is rough in the extreme. Tussocks, rough grass, peat hags and glutinous mud all combine to slow you down; and physically it is every bit as tough as the climb up the clough. If you look across to your left you will see a large cairn on the crest. A number of these have been placed all the way along the edge and the walking is easy since it is void of soil and grass. By following these cairns you will eventually arrive at a wall which has a gate in it about 100 yards from the edge. Through the gate you will pick up a faint track made by a Land Rover and this becomes more pronounced as you proceed. Eventually this track will bring you to the wall at the "Big End" of Pendle and from a gate in it you can then back track to the summit cairn.

From the summit cairn make your way towards the "Big End" at the northern edge of Pendle. The wall across your path has a gate in it on your left and a stile on your right. It is better to go over the stile as this points the way by means of a clearly defined broad track which begins to descend diagonally downwards. Soon you will come across a spring which gushes forth, known locally as Robin Hood's Well. It is due to the waterlogged millstone top grit meeting a band of shale which is not as porous and the water is forced out. The track after the spring becomes very narrow, being no more than a sheep track. It contours round for quite a way without gaining or losing any height until it meets a broad track downwards. Follow this and when the slope decreases turn away from Pendle and make your way for a stile to be seen ahead in a wire fence. From here a more distinct track appears leading straight down the hill across boggy ground, crossing three more stiles, to eventually emerge at the road which links Downham village with Annel Cross.

Walk downhill along the road to where it bends to the right in about 150 yards. On your left a gate opens on to a grassy lane bordered on either side by walls. An afforested belt of conifers on your left eventually gives way to open ground rising up to Downham moor. About ½ mile along this track following a wall on your right brings you round the back of Hook Cliff Farm. Through a gate here a more distinct roadway leads you on to Barkerfield. Just before Barkerfield a broad grassy path leads upwards and left behind the buildings and on to Moorside. Crossing a footbridge, go into and through the farmyard, and then follow the double concrete roadway until it meets a road leading off to the right. Follow this downhill and where it meets a road from the left continue straight ahead towards Worsaw Hill.

A sharp bend in the road to the right is the point where you go through a gate and follow the hedge on your right down to Worsaw Farm. Go through the farmyard and through a gate on your left. A broad track leads you on the right of a stream towards some tall trees and a stile.

From here the route is fairly obvious crossing two more stiles and then making for a gateway in a stone wall. Here you go through a stile and over a bridge into a very muddy lane which brings you back to the start of your walk at Worston.

Walk 9

The Round of Stang Top from Whitehough

Grade—Easy.
Distance—About 4 miles—Boots are not required.
Time—about 2 hours.

ABOUT a mile from Barley on the Nelson road, a sign on the riverside of the road proclaims the lane leading to Whitehough Camp School. Take your car down the paved slope, over the bridge, and past Whitehough Grange which was formerly Barley Youth Hostel, and ahead you will find ample space for parking.

A gateway here passes through the farmyard on its way to the Camp School, but your route lies along the path running parallel with the river for about 100 yards beyond this gateway. Here on your right a wooden swing gate leads into a small field which is terminated by a stile. Over this stile, another appears in a few yards leading you into a field behind the cottages at Whitehough.

Directly ahead is a broad expanse of conifer trees with a track leading through the centre. Go up the slope and through the gap to emerge from the trees before two gates side by side. At the side of the left hand one, a narrow rickety rustic gate gives access to a field. Turn left. The path makes across the field to the right hand corner of the conifers ahead. Beyond this a wooden gate in a wall, followed by a stile in a second wall lie in the same direction; and then the path curves round the side of the hill to the right.

Once over the crest of the rise, the path levels off and follows the wallside ahead to the righthand corner where an iron gate stands next to a stile. Care must be taken here not to get into the wrong field. Having crossed the stile follow the wallside and hawthorn trees on your left down to the lane connecting Barley with Black Moss Reservoirs.

Turn right and follow the lane to the end of the first reservoir. Here it takes a right hand bend to curve around the boundary wall of the Upper Reservoir at the top of which, it passes between two walls to cross a bridge. Continue along the lane following the feeder stream on your right until you come to the road.

Go along the road to your right, and look for an iron swing gate immediately past the buildings of Lower Black Moss Farm. This takes you along the wallside at first in the general direction of the wind pump ahead on the slopes of Stang Top. Leaving the wall go

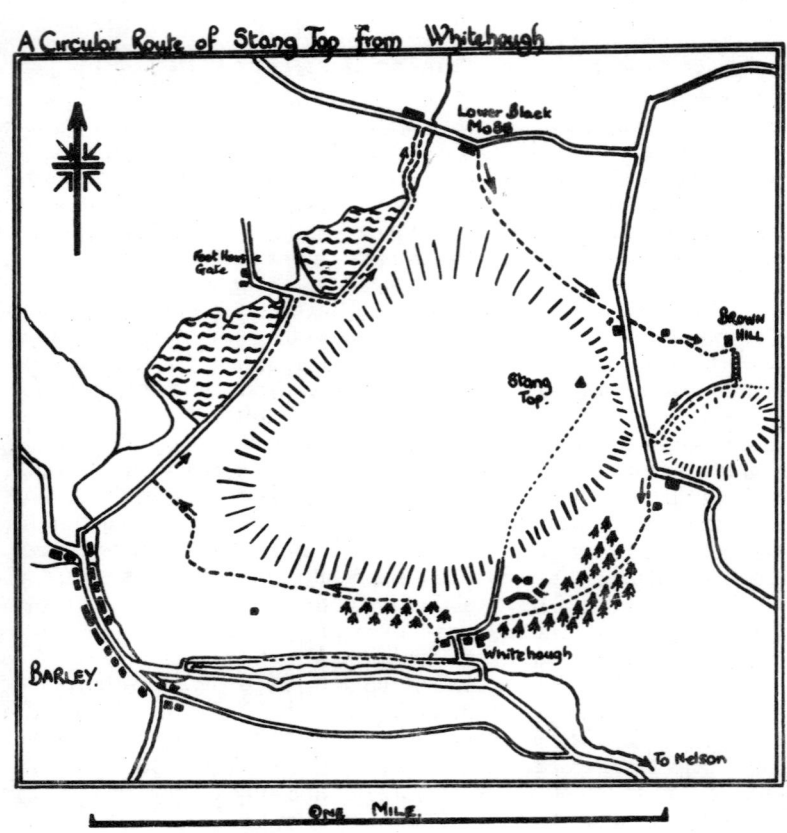

A Circular Route of Stang Top From Whitehough

Lower Black Moss

Foot Houses Gate

Stang Top.

BROWN HILL

BARLEY.

Whitehough

To Nelson

ONE MILE.

across the rough moorland sedge to a stile in the middle of the wall, and from here make directly to the lefthand side of the wind pump where you will find the next stile leading you on to a minor road.

Almost immediately opposite a footpath sign reads "Hollin Top ½m. Roughlee 1m." Pass through the swing gate and make for the righthand end of a ruined building ahead. On rounding the corner of the building you will see a stile and across this a path strikes out slightly to the right in the direction of a telegraph pole in the centre of the field. Beyond this a stone stile leads you down the side of a wall on your right to Brown Hill Farm, meeting the lane which joins it here with the road. Turn right and follow the lane until you arrive at the minor road.

Turn left and go downhill to where the road bends and two tall trees stand prominently besides a narrow stile. Follow the track from this stile down the side of the wall on your left to a small cottage and a second stile. Turn right at the cottage and walk down the side of a belt of conifer trees for about 100 yards.

A stile here takes you through the woodland and the path goes in a straight line through the trees to pass on the left hand side of the Camp School buildings and eventually emerge onto a metalled road. Turn left down the road and within 300 yards you will pass through the farmyard of Whitehough and back to your car.

Walk 10 Pendle via Whinberry Clough

Grade—Strenuous—rough terrain, boots are necessary.
Distance—about 6-7 miles involving some 1,400 ft. of climbing.
Time—about 4 hours (not including stops).

The name Whinberry Clough is a name used by local ramblers and is not to be found on any map. The name given to this clough on the 2½ inch Ordnance Survey Map is Boar Clough, butI prefer to use the former as it conjures up memories of the many times that I have ascended Pendle by this route. It is a varied and interesting route, involving a safe easy scramble directly up the course of the stream, and nothing has given me greater pleasure than crunching through heavy snow in winter in order to slip and slither on the ice in the waterway. The final climb out of the bed of the stream on to the open top of Pendle to meet the arctic blast sweeping across the snowy wastes has chilled me to the marrow; yet left my spirit uplifted in a way that can only be experienced. I can only recommend it to you as a route not to be missed.

Barley is your starting point, and you will find a convenient park for your car besides the Village Hall opposite the bridge at the end of the village. From here go along the unmetalled road leading from the Village Hall to the Filter House of the Water Board, and follow this lane up hill to the first reservoir. Go along its banks beside the conifers on your right until you reach the end of the reservoir and have completed your first mile. The road continues to meet a second conifer belt at the end of which it passes through a gate and begins to climb up the hill towards a second gate.

Through this gate the road gives way to a rough Land Rover track which you continue to follow upwards until it begins to level off. Soon after this point the track begins to drop downwards, and here a slight track may be found striking off to the right. If you cannot find this track it does not matter, head off to the right of the path, and keep your height as you contour round the side of the hill, until you see ahead a sheep fold. Make for this and clamber through it to emerge on the other side of the wall. Here you will see a distinct path which follows the side of the hill until you reach a deep cleft cutting into the hillside on your right. This is Whinberry Clough and is instantly recognised by the solitary hawthorne tree standing like a sentinel on the left bank at a higher level.

Unless there is a lot of water cascading down the clough it is not

42

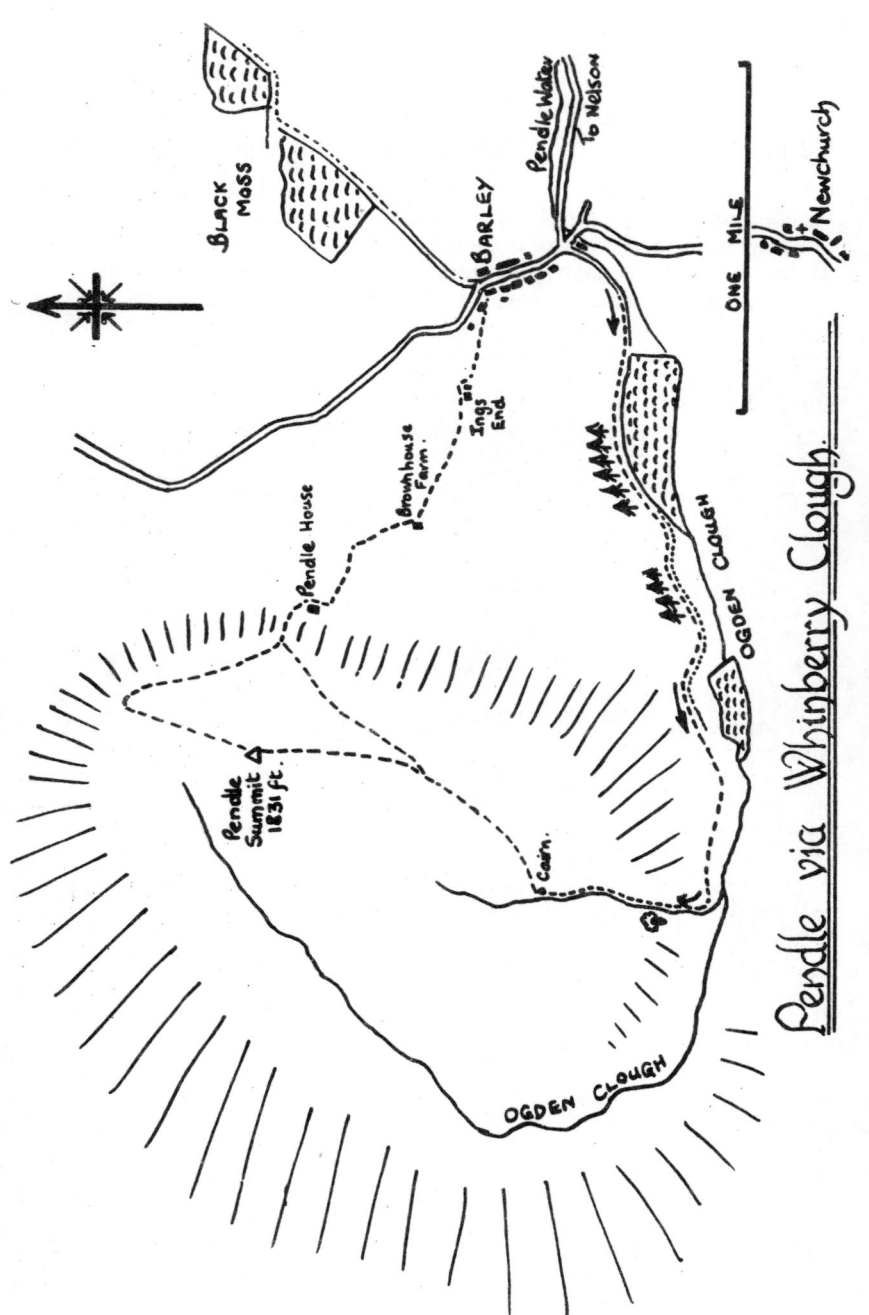

Pendle via Whinberry Clough.

only safe but exhilerating to walk up the bed of the stream. In winter when ice covers much of the rocks and icicles festoon the banks like gigantic tree roots the place is transformed into a fairyland. Follow the bed of the stream therefore, climbing gradually for about $\frac{1}{2}$ mile, until you see ahead a cairn sitting on a grassy lump on the skyline. Make for this and on arriving you will emerge from the stream onto the open moor of Pendle top.

From here to the summit there is no path. The going is rough under foot and if you carry a compass it should be set on 036 degrees magnetic. If you do not possess a compass then remember that you must continue to go uphill for you are still only at 1,500 ft. Make your way slightly to the right of the direction you had whilst climbing the clough and after about a mile you will see and be near to the summit cairn of Pendle.

The best descent from here is to continue along the edge of the hill in a northerly direction until you meet the wall which is the boundary of the flat summit and beyond which is the "Big End" of Pendle. Follow the wallside down to the right until you see a well built stile then follow the path leading from the stile back downwards to Pendle House Farm. The track is steep and stoney, but after dropping some 50 ft. from the edge, if you leave the track you will find below it and running parallel with it, a second grassy track, not as distinct, but certainly one which is much easier to follow.

Eventually arriving at Pendle House Farm turn right and go through the farm yard to a gate at the end. Through this turn left and follow the wallside on your left down. The path is fairly clear and leaves the wall through a gateway, drops down to a dell and then over a stile on your right to arrive at Brownhouse Farm. Go through the farm yard and through a stile to follow a stream on your right and a wallside on your left, down to Ings End. Here you will meet a distinct unmetalled roadway which you follow until you see a footbridge on your right. Go over the bridge and turning left follow the path which brings you out by the bridge and post office at the other end of Barley. From here you turn right and follow the road back to your car.

Walk 11   Churn Clough, Spence Moor and Cock Clough

Grade—Moderate—Strenuous under foot on Spence Moor. Boots are essential.

Distance—4 to 5 miles.

Time—allow at least 2 hours.

Equipment—It might be advisable to carry an Ordnance Survey map and a compass on this route as Spence Moor is wide and bleak should you be caught in mist.

NESTLING under the slopes of Goldshaw Booth, Sabden Fold is a small collection of cottages dominated by the Manor House. The peaceful scene, and the easy going of the first part of the walk will no doubt lull the unsuspecting walker into a false sense of security. From Churn Clough the going is tough, with a steepish ascent' no path, and rough tussock grass to be negotiated. For this reason I strongly recommend you to choose a good day and go armed with a ma p and compass.

Parking may be difficult at Sabden Fold so turn left along the road marked as a Cul de Sac and footpath to Sabden, and make your way to the first farm house on your right. This is situated at the foot of Cock Clough, the finish of the walk, and some spare ground for parking will be found just round the next corner.

Leaving your car, follow the metalled lane for about $\frac{1}{4}$ mile, and after passing a farm building on your left note that the road changes to a stony track. Go through the gate marked "No Road for Motorists—Footpath only" and later ignoring a footpath sign to Higham, proceed along the lane to the ruins of a farm building at Wood House Brook.

Cross the stream, and go through the gate on the otherside. The track now begins to ascend and then curves round to the right. At this point leave it and proceed up the steep embankment with the hedge and fence on your lefthand. On topping the rise you will see a stone stile ahead in a wall. This is followed by another stile besides a gate, and still in the same direction it leads to a broad grassy track which takes you on to Ratten Clough Farm.

A right of way exists through the farmyard leading to Sabden, but your path strikes out to the right of the buildings and follows the wallside on your left to a stone stile ahead. Across this stile the rough tussock grass and gradient carry you across a spur which leans out from Bank Hill. Where the gradient eases, the wall on your left meets another at right angles, and on the other side the ground slopes away into Churn Clough Reservoir. Do not cross this wall but turning right follow it closely downwards to a brook below.

Cross the brook via some stones, and then ascend the vague track, passing through bracken in summer, and following a fence line on your left. The track crosses a wall and makes for a steep sided

Cock Clough and Spence Moor

clough head. This is Churn Clough and at this point turn right and follow it uphill until you meet a broad track coming in from the opposite direction and leading to the remains of some ruined buildings called Craggs.

From Craggs climb up the hill with the stream on your left across rough tussock grass, first in a N.W. direction, and then curving round to the right as the bed of the tream alters its course. Your direction will change to a N.E. course, and still climbing, the rocky outcrop known as Deerstones, will appear before you and to your right. From here, the ascent is not as steep and follows the wallside on your left to a gate directly behind Deerstones.

Go through the gate. To your left the land falls away along a ridge leading to the Nick of Pendle, whilst ahead the broad back of Pendle rises majestically to its summit. Turn right and pick your way carefully over the tussocks and intervening morass on an Easterly course to ascend to the crest of what is Spence Moor.

No track is discernible, and because of the bleakness of the moor a strict compass course should be followed. The east course (090 deg.) will eventually bring you to the edge of an ever deepening valley separating Spence Moor from the massif of Pendle: this is Ogden Clough. Follow the compass and the rim of the moor until you begin to descend, at which point you may reset your compass to a 110 degree bearing.

Ahead and to your left are the reservoirs of Ogden Clough and the steep right hand bank is clothed in pines. Your direction, though still 110 degrees, makes a direct line for the righthand end of this conifer belt. You may be fortunate and pick up a faint footpath at this point, though don't be alarmed if you don't. Ahead now is a wall in the middle of which is a stone stile, and further down the slope you may be able to see a second wall and a track leading to it.

Cross the stile at the first wall and pick your way across boggy ground downwards and to your right. The second wall ahead of you dips away on its right over the brow of the hill. This is the beginning of Cock Clough and from the stile lies on a compass course of 158 degrees.

Just to the right of where the valley begins, the slope increases down to the remains of an old barn, only one wall of which remains standing. Pass this on the right and go down the wall side to enter the trees at the top of Cock Clough. A path follows the wall on the left and this leads you down to a spur. Descend this cautiously to the bed of the stream, and keeping on the left bank contour round the steep sided valley as the stream drops quickly away from you. A second wooded spur can be descended and this meets the stream, and here a wooden stile takes you over a fence and alongside the remains of a wooden shack that once sheltered Boy Scout Troops.

From here the path is quite clear and emerges from the trees above the farm. Make for the right hand side of the buildings alongside the Clough and from there back to the road and your car.

Walk 12   The 'Big End' of Pendle from Barley

Grade—Strenuous—in that a steep climb is involved.
Time—about 2 hours.
Distance—about 5 miles. Boots are essential.

PENDLE is climbed more often from Pendle House than from any other point, and if Pendle House represents the advanced camp then surely Barley must be the base camp. It is from Barley therefore that the hordes of walkers, ramblers and amblers set out on their expedition to climb, perspire, pause and gasp their way to the summit.

So popular is this walk to the inhabitants of the close lying industrial towns of N.E. Lancashire, that at Easter time in byegone days crowds flocked to Pendle, and Barley assumed the proportions of a Boom Town. Today the motor car takes these weekend walkers further afield, and there are no longer the numbers crawling their way to the summit. Yet I suppose it is rare that a day passes in the year without someone making this pilgrimage. Indeed in the many times that I have ascended its steep slopes I have never failed to meet some other kindred spirit; such is the popularity and magic of this hill.

Since Barley is so popular at weekends parking may be a problem, so might I suggest that this walk is undertaken on a weekday. The most convenient place to leave the car is besides the Village Hall close to the bridge as you enter Barley from Nelson or Burnley.

From here walk through the village passing on the right the Methodist Chapel, and on the left the village Post Office, to a sharp bend in the road. Here an unmetalled lane goes straight ahead and then turns right over a bridge crossing the stream. Take this lane and immediately you cross the bridge look for a stile on your left.

The path from the stile crosses a field leading to a gap in a wall on your right. Once through this gap you will be able to see the buildings at Over Houses, and the path leads to the right of them, to bring you out on to a lane at the right-hand side of a small bridge.

Turn left and cross the bridge. Ahead is a farm building, and the lane continues to its left. However, the path goes through the gate leading to the right of this building and through the farmyard. It emerges as a lane between two buildings and goes through a gate into an open field. Here the path curves slowly uphill to the left, to finally travel parallel with a wall on your right, which marks the boundary of the lower of Black Moss Reservoirs.

48

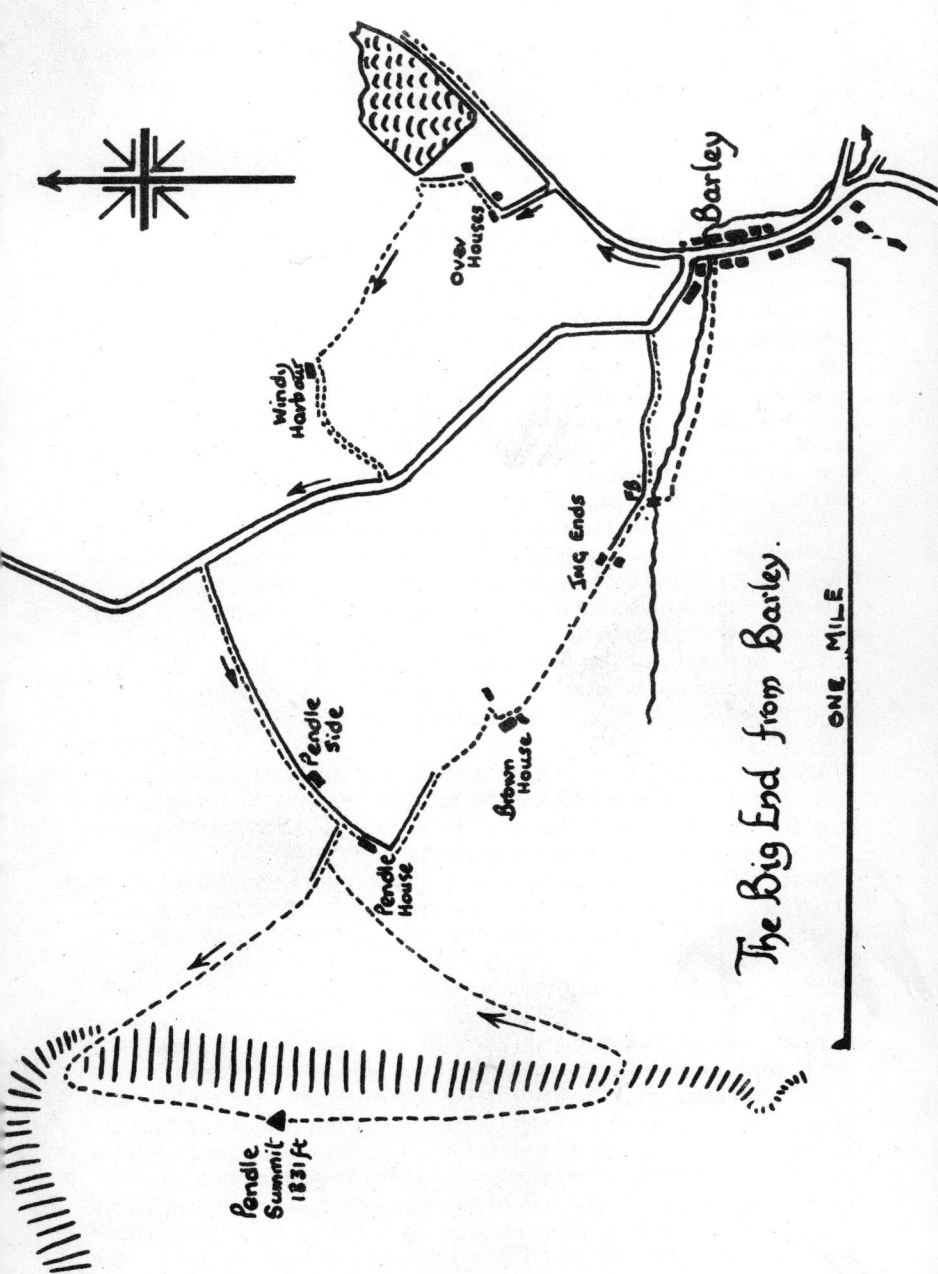

The Big End from Barley.

ONE MILE

Barley

Over Houses

Windy Harbour

Ing Ends

Pendle Side

Brown House ?

Pendle House

Pendle Summit 1831 ft

At the end of the wall, and the S.W. corner of the reservoir, is a gate with an iron swing gate next to it. Go through this and turn left. After about 20 yards you will pass through a gap into another field and here you must turn right and follow the hedge side up the gently sloping ground. Crossing two fields, the path enters a very overgrown lane leading to the buildings of Windy Harbour, with the "Big End" of Pendle acting as a backcloth.

On reaching the lane connecting Windy Harbour with the road, turn left and go to the lefthand side of the first building. Go through the gate and follow the wallside for about 50 yards. From here strike out to your left, first crossing a small stream, and then making for a stile to be seen in the wall ahead. Your path follows on your left the remains of a fence and is fairly obvious.

Across the stile turn right on the road, and then left about 50 yards higher up, to go over a cattle grid. This is the roadway leading to Pendle House and it is a Public Footpath. Follow it carefully and note that another road forks off to the left and leads to Pendle Side Farm. If you follow this lane you will have to retrace your steps.

Arriving at Pendle House, a stile on your right hand, or a swing gate nearer to the farm itself, takes you into a steep field which is the first part of the ascent. At the top of this field besides a wall is a gate and stone stile. Once across this stile follow the wallside on your right and where it ends a stony path ascends steeply to the skyline at the "Big End" of the hill; whilst a "cart-track" bears off to the left at a lesser angle and makes for the rim about halfway along Pendle's length. Whichever way up you decide on the return is by the other route.

Assuming that your choice is for the shorter but steeper route, look at it carefully and you will see that a track runs parallel with it but at a slightly lower level. This track is not well known, and is grassy besides being very much easier than the stony one.

About 50-100 yards from the end of the wall is the start to the easier grassy track. It leads off at first through bracken and then climbs steeply, but never-the-less more easily than its counterpart at a higher level which has to negotiate scree. Follow it until it finally reaches the crest of the hill at the "Big End". Ahead is a wall with a well-made stone stile in it which leads off towards Downham. Turn sharply to your left and following the edge of the hill make for the summit cairn and triangulation point some $\frac{1}{4}$ mile distant.

From the summit a further $\frac{1}{4}$ mile following the rim of the hill on a slightly descending route, brings you to the top of the cart-track. Turn sharply left and descend via this track, crossing the contours until you arrive in $\frac{1}{2}$ mile at the stone stile above Pendle House.

Make your way to the left of the building and through a swing gate. Turn right and go through the farmyard to a gate at the end of the lane. Here turn left and follow the wallside downhill across to a wooden swing gate. The track, though indisinct descends into an extremely muddy dell, which can be avoided by a slight detour to the left and then-returning to the path which leads to a stile over a wall.

Once across this stile you will see the buildings of Brown House Farm below and to your right. Follow the wall on your left to a lane and turning right pass through the farmyard and in front of the building to the left hand corner where a stile is situated. This points your way between the wall on your left and a stream on your right and in ¼ mile you will come to Ing Ends Farm to enter a lane.

Turn left in the lane and follow it downwards until you see a wooden bridge crossing the stream. Turn left after crossing the bridge and follow the stream on your left back into Barley village close by the Post Office.

Walk 13   Weets and Wheathead from Blacko

ONE of the most outstanding landmarks in the surrounding countryside is Blacko Tower. No matter where you are it acts like a beacon catching your eye, pinpointing your gaze, and giving direction to your view. It was built by J. Stansfield in 1890, was restored in 1950 and since then has had to be repaired due to vandalism. If you see the farmer at Stansfield House Farm he will readily give his consent for you to go up to it.

Armed with this permission your path starts at Blacko Bar opposite Blacko Laiths Farm. Here a gate leads you into a field and directly confronting you is a carved stone cross inscribed "Blacko Cross." I suspect this is of recent origin and not a true monastic cross. The track leads up the side of a wall for about quarter of a mile, and when you arrive at a tall tree you can then strike out directly for the tower. A stile has been purposely built to cross the wall and in the entrance of the tower a plaque exonerates the owner from any liability should an accident happen on his land. Climbing the winding staircase in the gloom of the interior you will be startled by the sudden transition to bright sunlight at the top. The view from the battlements, however, is certainly worth the climb.

Grade—Fairly Strenuous.
Distance—approximately 9 miles.
Time—allow about 4 hours, possibly even more if stops are made on route.
Parking—Blacko presents some difficulty for car parking. I have used an area round the back of Blacko School but this is not really adequate. Further down the road a private car park belonging to an Inn may be used if permission is first obtained.

THIS walk begins about 300 yards down the hill from Blacko on the main road where a footpath sign reads "Blacko Hillside ½ mile", and leads up an unmetalled road to Brownley Park Farm. In the farmyard turn right and go through a gate, the path leading you alongside a wall. In approximately 100-150 yards the track crosses a stile in the fence and then continues in a straight line for Black Hillside Farm. Go to the left round the back of the buildings and carry on until you reach a line of hawthorne trees crossing your

The Weets and Wheathead from Blacko.

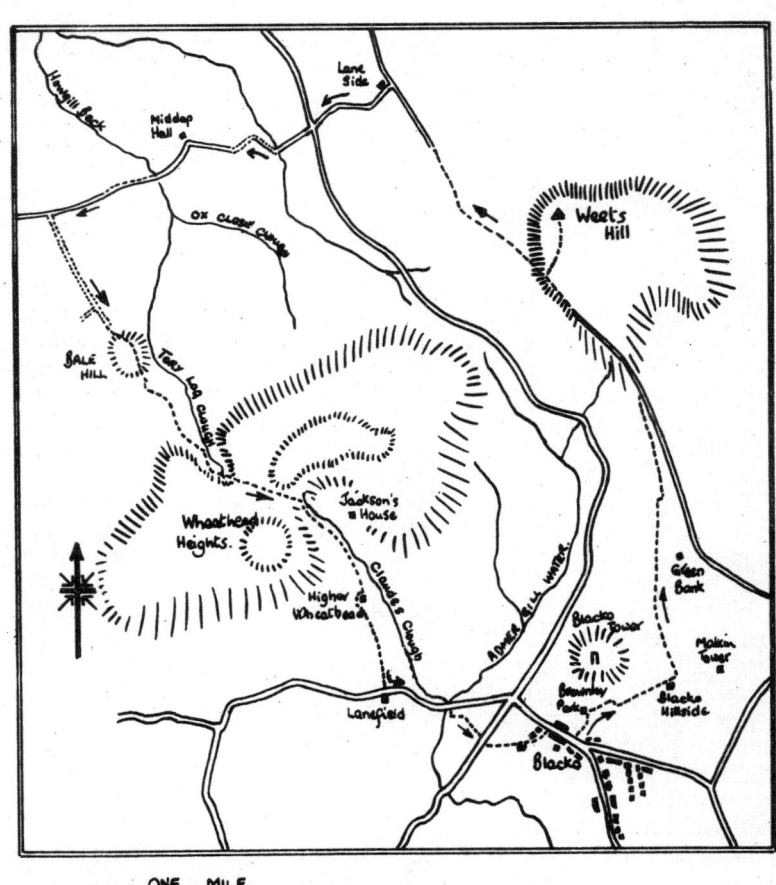

Lane Side

Hazel Back

Middop Hall

Ox Close Clough

Weets Hill

Bale Hill

Tree Leg Clough

Jackson's House

Wheathead Heights.

Green Bank

Higher Wheathead

Clarkes Clough

Admergill Water

Blacko Tower

Malkin Tower

Lanefield

Blacko Hillside

Blacko

Brownley Park

ONE MILE.

53

path and leading up the hill. Follow these trees keeping them on your right until you come to the top of the field. A stile here takes you into a rough pastured field, and the path follows a copse of trees and a wall on your right in a straight line for about half a mile. Ignore a stile crossing the wall on your right for this only leads to Green Bank Farm and continue in a straight line to the end of the field. Here a gate ahead comes into view and a stile on its right takes you over to the other side of the wall. Now follow, still in the same direction, as before but on the other side of the wall. A natural drainage channel follows the path and after crossing two stiles you will find the path converging with Coal Pit Lane or Gisburn Old Road. Ahead of you is a clump of trees and if you make directly for them you will see a wooden gate leading into it. This gate has been tied up firmly but this is the correct exit of the footpath.

Once on Gisburn Old Road, a metalled surface, follow it until you arrive at Stoops House. This is passed on the right and going through a gate you find you have left all roads and sophisticated means of travel behind.

Ahead is a wilderness of tufted grass, bog and moorland which has to be traversed. First however, let me plead that at this point you digress and taking some time from your allotted programme, turn right once through the gate at Stoops House. Now make your way upwards to the skyline following the wallside and after about 300 yards you can strike off directly to the "trig point" at Weets Hill. I can assure you there is no better view point in the whole of Pendleside, even though its height is only a modest 1,250 ft.

Retracing your footsteps to the gate at Stoops House, you now have to find your own way across the Weets. There is no track but I suggest you aim to travel in a roughly parallel line with the wall on your left hand at a distance of about 100 yards. After about ¼ mile a faint track will be seen making for a fence with a stile in it. Cross this and follow the wallside until you pick up the lane. This is the continuation of Gisburn Old Road so follow it until you reach some habitation on your left called Lane Side.

For a mile and a half or so the path follows a metalled road which tends to be unpleasant in hot weather to walk on, but it is a lane where you will meet no cars and it winds delightfully through some very beautiful stretches. Turn left, therefore, at Lane Side and follow the road until you come to the main Nelson-Gisburn road in about ¾ mile. Go directly across this road and through the metal gate on the other side to drop downwards still following the metalled road. You will eventually pass Middop Hall which is now a farm, and will no doubt want to stop to examine more closely the mullioned windows and sturdy architecture. Beyond the hall the road leads to Middop Bottoms, a most beautiful picnic spot where you can sunbathe by the side of the stream and dreaming wistfully drift into slumber.

Awakening guiltily you should now attempt to make up time by puffing up the hill to the farm on your left called Whytha. Just beyond this, about 100 yards or so, an unmetalled bridle path leads uphill to your left. This is your route. It climbs steadily crossing from the lush soft fields of Middop to acid moorland and peaty soils. In half a mile the straight double path turns right leading to some buildings at Higher Gills. Ahead is a gate, pass through this and follow the wallside on your left. The cart track turns leftwards but still following it strike up over Bale Hill.

Over the crest of Bale Hill the contours flatten out slightly and a stone wall crosses your path. An open gateway can be seen with a stile about 25 yards to its right. Make for the open gateway, not the stile which leads you into some very boggy ground, and follow the wallside on your right for about 200 yards to pick up another stile ahead. Across this your path leads to another wall on your left and a water drainage cleft with the unusual name of Tory Log Clough. Climb the contours by its side until you reach a stile at the top. Across this your path strikes out more or less in a straight line crossing a ridge which leans out northwards from Wheathead Height until you see another wall. A good stone stile takes you across this and Blacko Tower comes distinctly into view. At this point you will have reached about 1,150 feet and the highest part of the return route. From the stile your path follows in line with Jackson's House Farm and the beacon of Blacko Tower. On the skyline on your left you will be able to make out the outline of Weets Hill. The path is now more distinct and crosses downhill towards a clough, at the top end of which is a cattle grid and stile leading to Jackson's House. Below this and to the right however, is a gate which will take you down alongside the right hand side of the clough to Higher Wheathead Farm. On arriving at this farm keep to the right of the buildings and then pick up a broad double track which leads you down to the main road at Lanefield.

On arrival at the road turn left and travel about $\frac{1}{4}$ mile downhill to a bridge which crosses Admergill Water. Here two footpath signs are in evidence, the second one across the bridge being the one which you should take, for it reads "Blacko Village $\frac{3}{4}$ mile". Across the stile the path leads down some steps, then skirting through some trees alongside the river bank emerges into an open field. Turn left and almost back on yourself here, and make your way upwards alongside some holly bushes to the crest of a slight incline. A natural gateway between hedges points your way, then along side a hedge on your left until you reach the main Blacko-Roughlee road. Across this road a footpath sign directs you to Blacko Village via Spout Houses in $\frac{1}{2}$ mile. Following this path eventually takes you through a farm yard and from thence to the main Gisburn-Nelson road at the top end of Blacko village and finally to your car.

55

Grade—Easy. Boots are not required unless it is muddy.
Distance—about 4 miles.
Time—allow about 2 hours.

THERE are certain points of interest in a district which demand exploration and Noyna Rocks is such a well known landmark. It is situated to the N.E. of Pendleside within easy reach of Colne, and Foulridge is the obvious starting point.

As you approach from Colne turn right along Blenheim Terrace at the "Hare and Hounds" Inn, and park your car in the vicinity of "The New Inn" about 100 yards further along. Retrace your steps along Blenheim Terrace and look for an overgrown entrance to a lane which leads up hill on the opposite side to the terraced houses. Go up this lane and cross the wooden stile at the other side of the field. The path follows the fence on your right hand crossing three stiles and fields in a straight line and passing some 100 yards away from Lower Broach Farm on your left. Cross the next field diagonally though still in the same general direction as before, and make for a short stone wall which appears to be stranded in a hedgerow ahead. Here is a stone stile through which you pass with another some 50 yards distant. Now your way crosses a field with a farm on your right hand, and an unmetalled road or lane directly ahead.

Once on the unmetalled lane walk down it towards the Upper Reservoir which is crossed by the lane over a causeway. The lane now begins to climb up towards Castle Road and where it reaches a bungalow on your right hand you will discover a stone stile on your left. From here a well defined path follows a fence and then a stone wall curving downwards towards Lower Clough Farm. Follow the unmetalled farm road into the farm yard, turn right and at the end of the buildings right again through a gate. Go round the end of the building and make straight across for a copse of trees. A very concealed stile here leads to a footbridge crossing a stream and over another stile at the other side. It is very easy to miss your way here as no path can be seen. From the footbridge climb up hill alongside a line of trees and a drainage ditch on your right for about 100 yards. From here is seems natural to follow a hedgerow leading off to the left but look carefully for a small wooden stile in the corner which takes you into another field. Follow the side of the field uphill and towards the stile which can now be seen on the skyline a little to the left of the righthand corner of the field. Once through this stile another becomes apparent crossing a stone wall on your right just ahead. From here the path crosses diagonally making for the top righthand corner, and when you reach it, Moss Houses comes into view on your right. Following the top wall of the next field go through

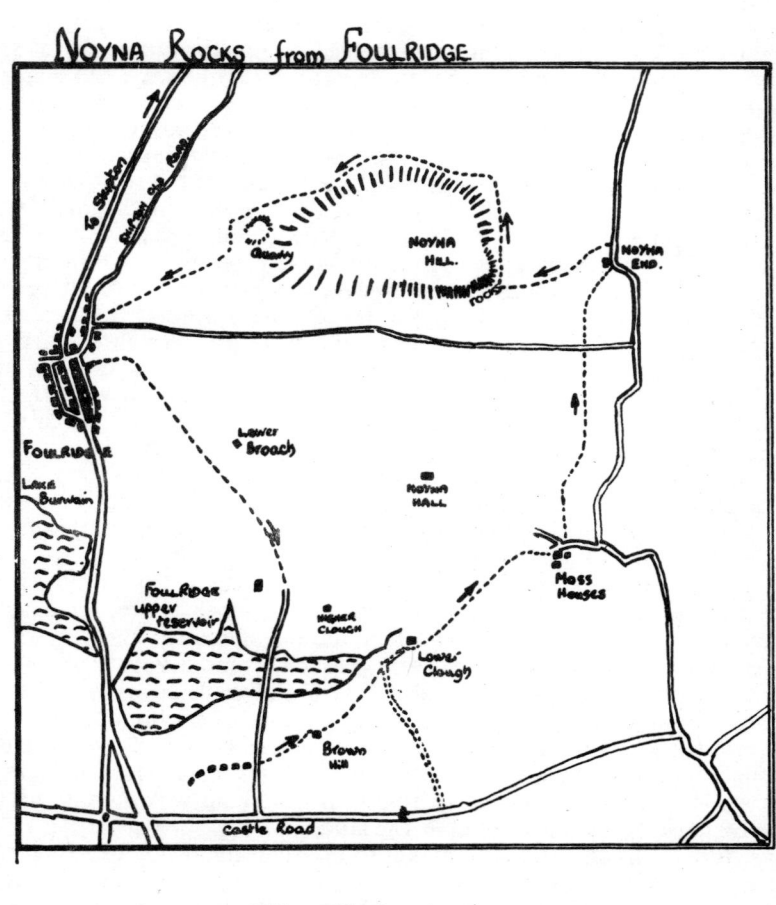

NOYNA ROCKS from FOULRIDGE

ONE MILE

an iron swing gate and then through a five barred gate to enter the farmyard area at Moss Houses.

Turn left and go round the end of the first building where you will meet another lane coming in on your left from Noyna Hall, continue and opposite the last building at Moss Houses you will see a stone stile. The path follows the remains of a line of Hawthorne trees until these peter out. Here two tracks seem to diverge, one bearing off to the left towards a wall, and the other leading ahead and slightly to the right. Follow the latter course and make your way directly to a stile about 300 yards distant and in the direction of some buildings. Once in the next field a stile will be seen in a stone wall to the left of Cornshaw Brook Farm and this brings you out on to the road running parallel with Noyna Bottoms. Directly across the road another stile leads to a path which first follows the wall on your left and then strikes out for the farm buildings of Noyna End ahead. The stile which leads to the road is to the immediate right of these buildings.

Once on the road turn left and passing the farm look carefully for a stile at the top of the banking just past the last building. Go through this stile and follow the wall on your left going through a narrow exit to the field in the corner. Turn left here and go over the stile in front of you, then turn right and follow the wallside on your right until you can see two stiles ahead which lead you direct to Noyna Rocks.

The rocks are composed of typical Millstone Grit and lie at a high angle of dip. If you have Vibram soles on your boots and the rock is dry you can spend some time here recapturing your youth scrambling over them.

When eventually you tear yourself away from the rocks the path you follow goes up hill at right angles to the path you approached by. Follow the wall on your left hand and make for the very top lefthand corner of the field. Here you will come across a wooden stile, cross it and turn left, and follow the wallside on your left descending slightly. Cross a stone stile in the corner about 300 yards from the last one and continue to follow the wallside down. Eventually you will reach the corner of the field but there is no stile here, turn right and follow the wall now downhill until you come to a hawthorn tree besides which is the stile.

Across this stile the path makes to the right hand side of a quarry and from here you will see the remains of a quarry track leading down to an iron gate. Go through this and turn left, climb up the slope on your left, ignoring the fact that the quarry path leads straight down. Once on the crest you will see an open gateway through a stone wall, go through this, turn right and descend towards an iron gateway ahead. The path is not too clear but stretches out in a straight line now back towards Foulridge emerging eventually in the corner opposite the village school. From here follow the road downhill and back to your car.

Walk 15 White Moor from Higherford

Grade—Moderate. Boots not essential.
Distance—about 7 miles.
Time—about 3-3½ hours.

ON the Northern edge of the Pendleside district is a tract of land called White Moor. It is a bleak stretch of rough country rising to 1200 ft, privately owned, and developed as a Grouse Moor. There are a number of footpaths crossing it, but most of them are private and only frequented by those hunting game birds. However, a grassy lane crosses the sloping ground called Lister Well Road and the name is of some interest. Lister is a local old English name for a man working in the dyeing of fabric for the textile trade; and the site of Lister Well is marked on the adjoining sketch map. As there is no evidence of a dwelling here, how came this well by this name? Here is indeed a problem that can only be solved by delving into old historical records, and should prove an interesting piece of research.

About 200 yards above Higherford Bridge, where the road forks left to Blacko and right to Barnoldswick, is the start to the walk. Take the right hand fork and immediately turn right again up a small gravel lane called Francis Avenue, to find some spare ground ahead where you can park your car.

Leaving the car turn left and go on to the end of the lane, through an iron swing gate into a field. The path goes diagonally across the field making at first for the lock house on the other side of the canal, and then heading to the right to a footbridge. Cross this and turn left on the towpath, to follow it for approximately one mile until the canal disappears at the "Mile Tunnel".

Of recent years the canal has enjoyed renewed activity. Where barges pulled by horses once plied loads of coal to various industrial towns, now gaily painted pleasure boats carry holiday makers through the many locks that exist between here and Skipton. The atmosphere of affluence extends to the lock house, for now it is no longer the dingy little house standing besides the canal, but a brightly painted building serving as ship's office, shop, and meeting point for the fresh water navigators of Britain's inland waterways.

This is easy walking with no problems of route finding, and one can concentrate on enjoying the countryside as the towpath gently winds its way to Blakey Bridge. Beyond this, and then a second

59

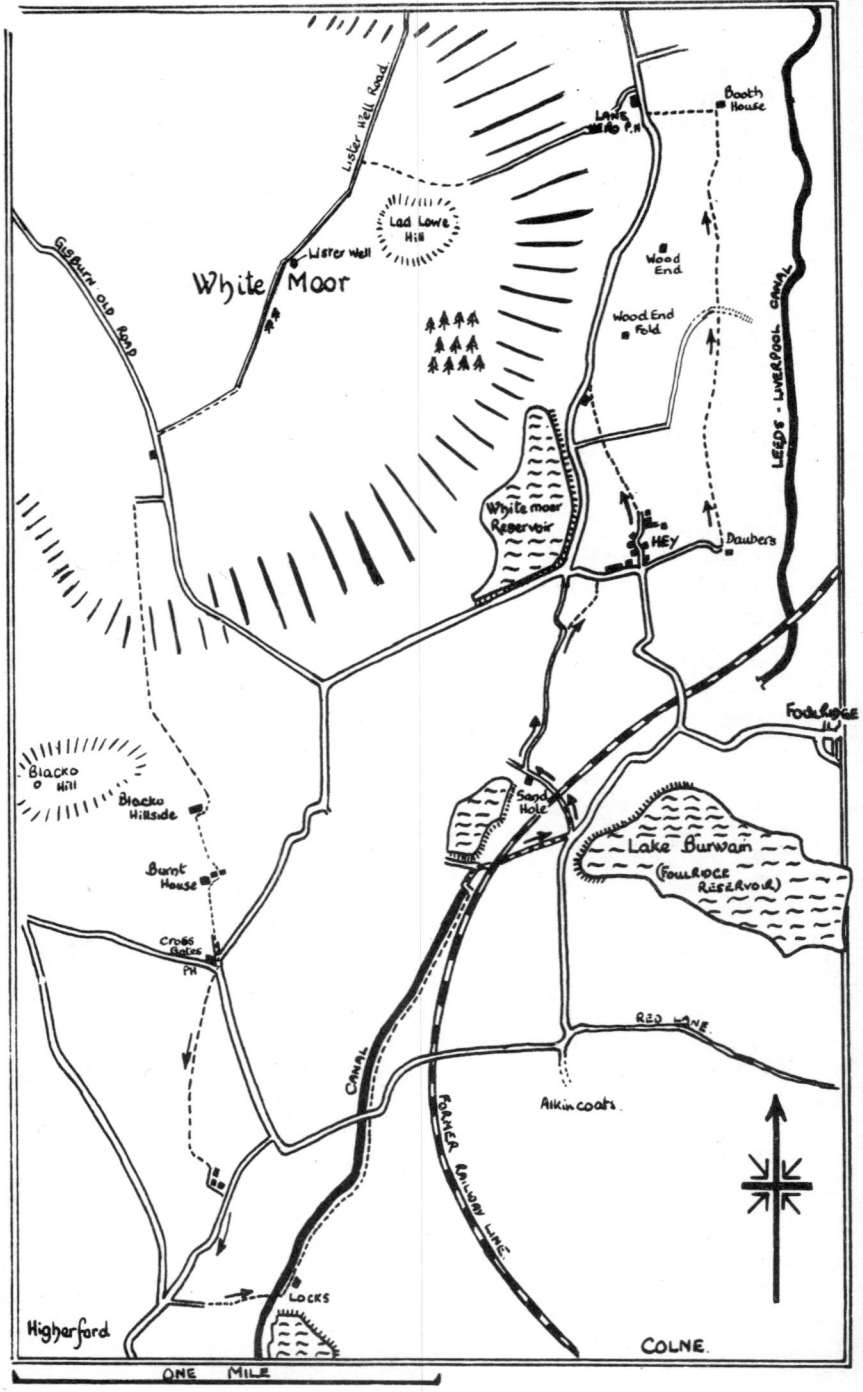

bridge, the canal enters a straight stretch leading directly into the open mouth of the "Mile Tunnel". Here is is swallowed and travels underground to re-emerge in one mile at Foulridge. Here, the barge horse had to be taken round by the lane; whilst the bargeman lay on his back, and with his feet on the roof of the tunnel, walked the barge through the darkness to Foulridge.

Follow the towpath to the beginning of the tunnel and then ascend to the right and cross over the bridge to enter a lane. This lane is crossed by another one at right angles to it in 300 yards. Turn right here and go across the remains of the railway track. Immediately across, a lane on your left, leads in a straight line to Foulridge Reservoir, now rejoicing in the new name of Lake Burwains since it became a popular site for a Yachting Club.

Emerging through a gate from the lane onto a metalled road, you will notice a footpath sign on your left reading "White Moor Bottom ¾ mile" This points your way along a lane which recrosses the railway track, and then ascends slightly passing a building on your left called Sand Hole. Ahead the lane continues towards another farm, Moss House, but on your right an overgrown grassy path disappears beneath a multitude of leafy boughs. This is your route, and threading your way gingerly through the first 25 yards of nettles, you will find the path opens out beneath a canopy of tree branches intermingled and entwined in loving embrace. Continue along this path, passing a building called Ball House; and now more in the open, climb the gently ascending lane until it turns sharply left. Here a stile on your right leads you alongside a wall to eventually emerge on to a farm road. Go left along it to the main road in a couple of hundred yards.

Turn right along the road, and passing a few houses make for the first sharp bend. Here on your left two lanes leave the road. One strikes out towards Daubers, whilst the other, the one on your immediate left passes through a farmyard at Hey, and continues until some new buildings appear ahead. Take the latter lane, and turn right when you arrive at the new buildings, to follow a narrow lane down to a farm building which you pass on the left. Here a footpath leads to Hey Fold Farm and a farmlane. Turn right on this metalled surface and follow it round to the left. After ½ mile look carefully for a footbridge which crosses the stream called County Brook.

Once across the bridge, a footpath follows the wall, then crosses a field to the left of a building. Still continuing in the same direction cross two more fields to meet a lane linking the main road with Booth House Farm. Turn left and follow the wallside to the road to emerge opposite the Lane Head Public House.

Just beyond the Inn, a footpath sign reading "Guisburn Old Road" points your way up a steepish lane which at first winds left then right. This leads towards a farm building which is passed by going through a small wooden swing gate and the lane continues for about 200 yards to be terminated by a metal five barred gate. Go through this on to the open hillside. Ahead on the skyline a wall runs along the crest of the hill and is broken by two gates. The one on your right is the one you should aim for, and passing through it follow the wallside until you come to Lister Well Road.

Turn left along the lane which is overgrown and bounded on either side by stone walls, and continue for approximately half a mile along this bridle path. It is eventually terminated by a rusty old metal gate, and once through this the path follows a wallside until it emerges into Guisburn Old Road.

Turn left and walk downhill passing Peel's House Farm on your right, and in another 100 yards turn right into an overgrown lane besides a small copse of trees. At the end of this lane turn left once over the stile, to follow the wallside through two fields and for a distance of about ½ mile. Go over the stone stile at the bottom corner of the second field and carefully negotiate the boggy section before making downhill towards Blacko Hill Side Farm alongside a line of hawthorne trees. Enter the farmyard by means of a gate and look carefully for a wooden stile on your left leading off to Burnt House Farm. Cross two fields and then pass between two narrow fence lines to enter the concreted area of Burnt House. Go between the buildings and through a gate on your right into the driveway. This is a Public Right of Way should you be questioned by the farmer and you have every right to make for the road ahead by going down his drive.

On meeting the road, a few yards further on will bring you to the Cross Gaits Inn and directly across from it two footpaths signs vie for your attention. Choose the one on the left which reads "Higherford ¾ mile" and going over the stile follow the telegraph poles diagonally across the field to a stile in the opposite corner. From here the path goes across another field making for a distinct copse of tall trees where another stone stile will be found. Go over it, and on emerging from the trees make for a gap in the wall on your right which is the entrance to a new housing site.

Follow the road between the houses and at the end turn left to meet Barnoldswick Road. Turn right and retrace your steps to Francis Avenue which leads to Grange Avenue where you parked your car.

Pendle View and Downham

Water Meetings

Roughlee Hall (*Lancashire Evening Telegraph*)

Downham Village (*Lancashire Evening Telegraph*)

Bronte Parsonage (*Lancashire Evening Telegraph*)

Ponden Hall

Foster's Leap

Bronte Waterfall

BRONTË COUNTRY WALKS

Walk 16   Penistone Hill and the
              Bronte Waterfall from Haworth

Grade—Moderate.
Distance—About 6 miles.
Time—about 3 hours.

HAWORTH village is a curious contrast of old and new, divided by the valley of Bridgehouse Beck. On one side are the rather drab rows of houses of nineteenth century origin; whilst on the other narrow cobbled streets and quaint old fashioned buildings climb upwards towards the Church and Vicarage where the Brontes lived, worked and played. At weekends hundreds of devotees descend on the village thronging the church, main street and museum, absorbing the atmosphere which the local residents have been careful to preserve. Discreet antique shops alternate with small bookshops and tea rooms. The bustling populace, yields a picture which could have come straight from a history book. This is the charm of Haworth, a glimpse into a previous century which only requires the taffeta and bonnets, the tall hats and mutton chops to complete the setting. This was the world of the Bronte family.

No doubt Penistone Hill and the Bronte Waterfall described below were the playground of the Bronte children, and it was in the atmosphere of the Vicarage and the surrounding countryside which led them to invent their childhood romances which were the prelude to their later literary genius. At this point I would recommend a visit to the Vicarage Museum which will tell the reader far more about the Bronte family than ever I can relate in this short introduction.

At the top end of the village, just off the main street, is a largish car park; conveniently placed for immediate access to the Vicarage Museum. Leave the car park, and once on the main street turn right and wend your way towards the church. Here a public footpath sign points the way to Haworth Moor by going round the righthand side of the church. A further sign takes you through the graveyard at the back of the church to meet a narrow lane passing between iron railings.

In about 300 yards a sharp right hand bend leads into a wider gravelled roadway, and this leads uphill to emerge on to a minor metalled road. Directly opposite is a drainage ditch on the open

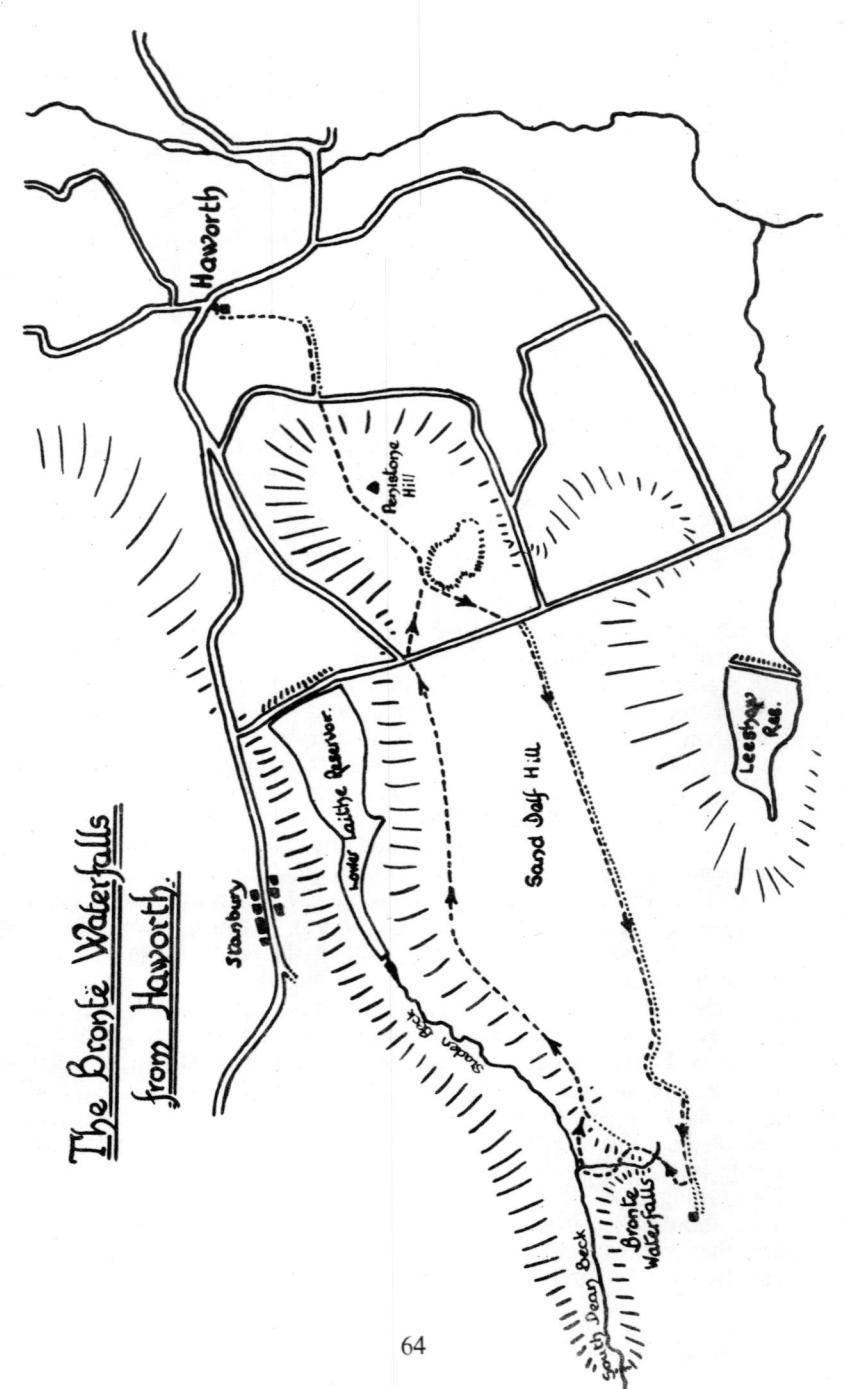

The Brontë Waterfalls
from Haworth.

Haworth

Penistone Hill

Lower Laithe Reservoir.

Stanbury

Sand Delf Hill

Leeshaw Res.

Sladen Beck

South Dean Beck

Brontë Waterfalls

moor, and a narrow footpath on the left of it makes towards some quarries on the skyline. Follow the path which makes for the right-hand side of the quarries and passes within a few yards of the triangulation point on Penistone Hill.

The summit of this hill is flat, and your direction is defined by the path which makes towards a boulder strewn area about 300 yards ahead. Here another quarry is encountered and skirting its edge drop down towards the Oxenhope-Stanbury road which crosses the moor at this point.

If you walk down to the lefthand side of the moor where a wall brings the road within bounds, you will find a gravelled roadway leading off on a compass bearing of 258 degrees magnetic. This roadway is marked as a Private Road but takes the walker for about $1\frac{1}{2}$ miles towards a residence on the upper moor by Harbour Hill. Follow this road, obtaining glimpses of Leeshaw Reservoir on your left as you pass over the gentle slopes of Sand Delf Hill. Continue along this roadway for almost its whole length until, nearing the residence, you see a gateway and cattle grid, as well as another Private Roadway sign. At this point turn right and leaving the road-way drop down to a little stream which you must cross. On the other side a faint track makes off on a compass bearing of 016 degrees magnetic linking a line of shooting butts. Recross the stream by means of a plank to where the path becomes more clear and follow it as it slowly curves around the hillside.

Ahead is the deep clough in which South Dean Beck flows towards Stanbury, whilst beyond on the farther bank derelict homesteads are evidence of a more prosperous time for hill farmers. Eventually the path comes out at the top of a steep gully, where the water tumbles and cascades downhill to meet the main stream in the valley bottom. This is the Bronte Waterfall.

Turn left and cross the rocks at the head of the gully to a steep little path that descends on the left side of the miniature cataract. In the valley bottom a footbridge carries pedestrians across onto the Ponden side of the valley and unless you wish to extend the walk do not cross it. Instead peruse the waterfall and gully and reflect on the stories that these surroundings could tell.

Now turn down stream and follow the bank of the stream slowly climbing out of the valley bottom. Eventually the path widens into a distinct roadway along which countless thousands must have travelled in order to view the waterfall and perhaps to go up to Top Withens. This pathway is followed now for about $1\frac{1}{4}$ miles until it emerges on the Oxenhope-Stanbury road just above Lower Laithe Reservoir.

Across the road and to your right are the quarries you passed over on your outward journey. Make your way to the lefthand side of them and pick up the path on the top of Penistone Hill which re-traces your steps back to Haworth.

Walk 17   Top Withens from Ponden Hall

Grade—Moderate.
Distance—about 6 to 7 miles.
Time—3½ to 4 hours.

PONDEN HALL is the official starting point to this walk, though you cannot park your car here. I would suggest that you turn off the Colne-Haworth road to cross the embankment of Ponden Reservoir, and then leave your car on the very wide lane which leads around the side of the reservoir to the Hall.

This 17th century building is a working farm, but Mrs. Dyson finds time to cater for Pennine Way travellers who, leaving Edale at a weekend, generally arrive at Ponden by Tuesday or Wednesday evening. Other walkers, and those Bronte admirers wishing to see the Hall which is thought to be the Thrushcross Grange of Emily's Wuthering Heights, are made welcome for either a hot or cold meal providing prior notice has been given.

Inside are large rooms with stone mullioned windows, gigantic fireplaces and oak beams. One bedroom actually boasts six double beds and two single ones for parties of walkers who do not mind sharing accommodation; whilst the main room has an atmosphere created by the antique furniture and stuffed animals.

The first part of the walk, from Ponden to Top Withens, follows the Pennine Way. Leave the corner of the embankment of Ponden Reservoir by a narrow lane leading up and around the back of a dwelling house with the unusual name of "Rush Isles". This lane leads into one of the muddiest sections I know, so negotiate its upper reaches with care to eventually emerge on more solid ground at Buckley. Here a roadway curves off to the left, but cross the tussock grass and rushes to the end of a wall, and mount the steep slope by its side until you come to another lane. Here you go through a gate and to the end of the lane where a cairn marks the way for Pennine Wayfarers. Turn right at this cairn and follow the track all the way up to Top Withens in about 1½ miles.

Top Withens, thought to be the setting for the Wuthering Heights of the novel is now no more than a ruin. Ten or so years ago it was still presentable as a building but the rapid decay that has taken place during the last decade is, I am sure, not all Nature's handiwork. No doubt it was here that the Bronte children romped and made up

Ponden Hall to Withens.

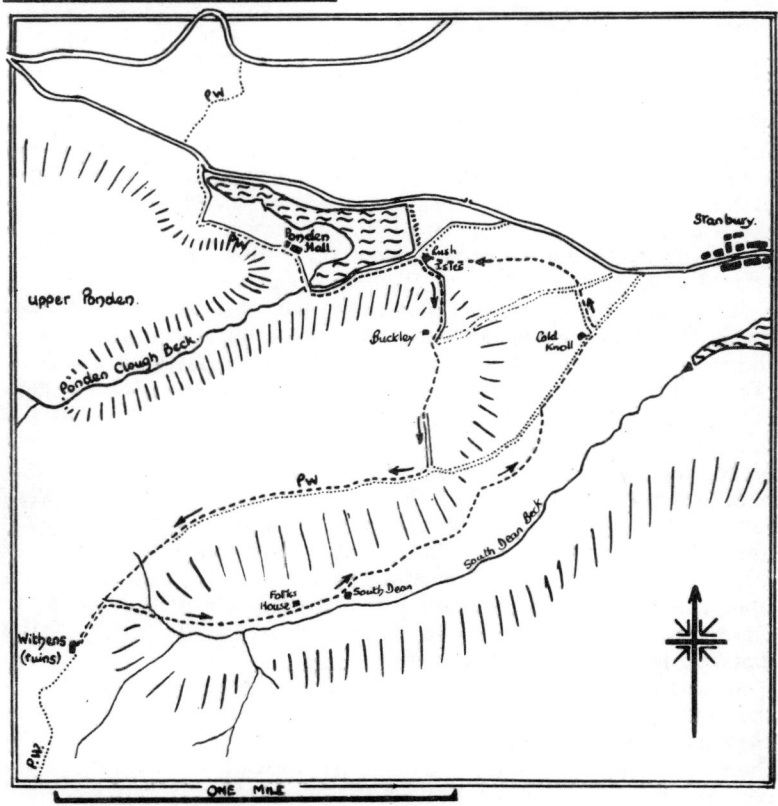

their imaginary stories that seem to have been a release for their creative talents during their childhood. A plaque has been cemented to the wall of the ruin explaining the buildings' association with the Brontes, and it is to this spot that hundreds of pilgrims wend their way every summer.

You will have noticed that during the last 1½ miles the track has deteriorated to almost a "sheep track" on its arrival at Top Withens. It continues up to the crest of the hill and down the other side as the Pennine Way, dropping down past Upper and Lower Walshaw Dean Reservoirs to meet the Widdop road. Though this is not your route, I can thoroughly recommend this walk to you, if you are able to place a car at either end of the walk, for this is real moorland walking with a sense of adventure.

From Top Withens retrace your steps for about 200 yards and then turn right down the side of a low stone wall, to drop towards the valley below. Continue along the track which runs parallel with South Dean Beck, until you come to Fork's House. Across the valley to the south, you will see the gully down which cascades the Bronte Waterfall, and a track leads down to a footbridge in the bottom should you wish to visit it.

If not, continue your way along the path, passing Fork's House and at the corner of a wall ahead, turn right along a path way leading to another building called South Dean. This path carries on, following a wallside on your left, to emerge onto a double track which climbs slowly uphill. Go up the slope, and then turn right along the first pathway crossing your route. This leads into a lane which runs all the way back into Stanbury.

Follow this lane, which is now bordered on either side by a wall, for about a quarter of a mile until you come to a building on your left called Cold Knoll. Straight on leads to Stanbury, but two forks leave this track on your lefthand. Take the one which cuts back obliquely, the left hand one, and follow it until you arrive at Buckley. Once more negotiate the muddy lane to emerge at the corner of the embankment of Ponden Reservoir.

At this point I would suggest that the driver of the car takes it to the main road and turning left goes on to the end of the reservoir. Here he will see a large Pennine Way Route Board where he can park the car. In the meantime the passengers, instead of travelling in the car can set off to the left following the curve of the reservoir round to Ponden Hall. The driver having left the car can set off up the lane on the Pennine Way which crests a slight rise and curves to the left towards Ponden and his passengers.

Walk 18   The River Worth from Haworth

Grade—Easy.
Distance—about 3 miles.
Time—about 1½ hours.

HEATHER, tussock grass, sphagnum moss, rushes; are a common features of the peaty moors which border Haworth on the south and west. They call for warm clothing and a determination of spirit before setting out across them, and often your only reward are a pair of wet muddy feet. It is indeed a pleasure, therefore, to suggest a short walk from Haworth which covers an area of green fields, hedgerows and prosperous farms.

Leave your car in the main car park just off the top road at Haworth. Turn left from its exit onto the Stanbury road and walk along it passing the Baptist Chapel on your right and the Manse; and head for "The Old Sun Inn" at a bend in the road ahead. Directly opposite the inn, on the other side of the road, is a car park exclusively for the use of the patrons enjoying some of the bottled sunshine. The path begins at this point, travelling down the wallside on your left to become a broad but short grassy lane leading to a gate.

From here the way is apparent, though you may have to look carefully for the stiles. The path leads down to the right handside of a modernised farm building called Oldfield. Pass through the farm yard, and immediately beyond the last building is a wooden gate which appears to have never been opened judging by the state of the overgrown grassy lane beyond. However, cross the stile by its left, and walk down the lefthand side of Oldfield Lane. At the bottom end of the field it is possible to descend into the lane and walk down it to the river ahead.

The lane, muddy and overgrown in parts, arrives at the River Worth where a tributary stream, Sladen Beck, joins it. Here a picturesque little pack horse bridge takes you over to the other side where you must turn right along the river bank. Directly ahead about 50 yards distant are two solitary gateposts without a gate, and beyond a few trees and hedgerows mark the continuation of the lane on the opposite bank of the River Worth.

Once more, this grassy lane is too overgrown to actually walk in it, so follow it upwards on the left hand side. At the top lefthand corner of the field is a gate, which allows you to cross the lane so that you are on the righthand side of it. Follow it again, and then where it broadens out, drop into it and walk towards a copse of mixed deciduous hardwoods ahead. These hide a steep sided valley containing a rapidly flowing stream called Lamb Beck. Cross a

69

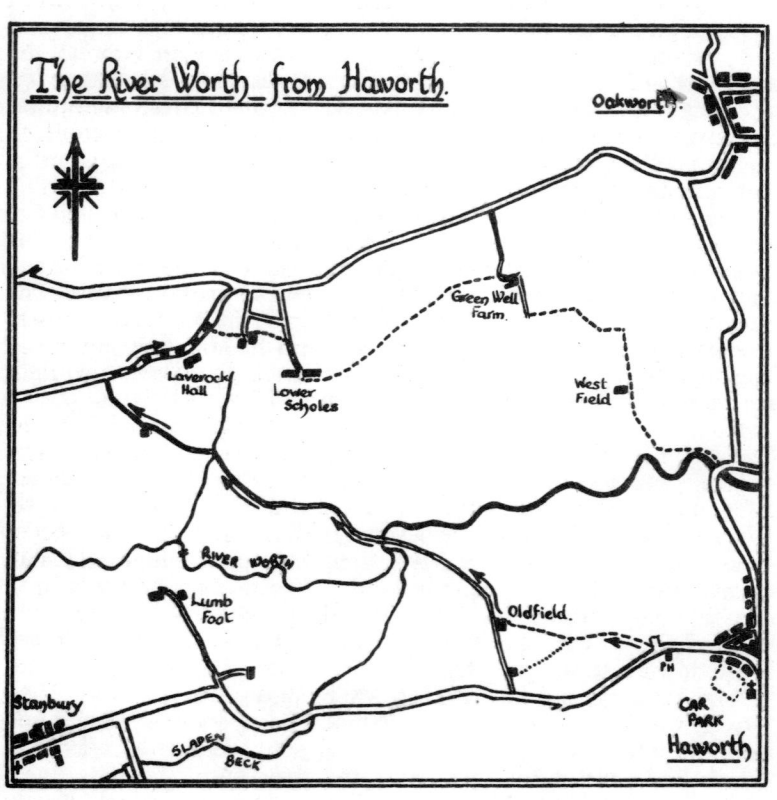

wooden stile to arrive at the perimeter of the trees where the lane curves off to the right. However, in the lefthand corner, a narrow wooden snicket allows you to enter the trees and the path curves first right then left, to cross the stream. This is a delightful spot, and such a contrast to the open moorland, that it is worth while pausing to admire the little waterfall, the deep V shaped cleft of the valley and the cosy atmosphere of the surrounding trees.

The remains of a wooden stile leads from the top of the waterfall to a grassy avenue bordered on either side by hawthorn trees, and this continues towards a farm building. Make your way to the righthand side of it into a farm lane which leads to the road. After about 100 yards along this lane go over a stile on your right, and crossing two fields emerge on to the road just before Laverock Hall.

The Hall has obviously been modernised in a tasteful way, and is worth while inspecting. Its architecture is typical of local building of the 16th and 17th century with mullioned windows and an entrance guarded by a stoutly studded oak door.

Walk along the road passing the Hall and at the bend, where stands an old fashioned gas lamp, go down to a narrow stile. The path makes for the lefthand side of the farm building ahead, crosses a lane, and over another stile to make for a building beyond called Higher Scholes. On emerging to the farm lane, by a gate, turn right and follow the lane down to the buildings of Lower Scholes.

Turn left and pass in front of the farm building at Lower Scholes. The lane leads into a field which is bordered on the right by some tall trees running parallel with the path. Cross two stiles in direct line, and then make diagonnaly across the next field towards a gate· Do not go through the gate for just beyond it in a few yards, another stone stile takes you over into a field, and the path follows the wall-side to a stile ahead by another copse of trees. Beyond these, in a straight line, is another stone stile leading into a lane. Turn right down the lane and pass round the back of Green Well Farm, going through a gate to follow the lane down to the bottom end of a field.

At the bottom end of the lane a broken gate bars your way. Here look carefully for a stile on your left which, once across, allows you to follow a wall on your right to the corner of the field. Here cross a low wall as the wooden stile is in a decrepit state.

The path cuts diagonally across the next field towards a wall end, and following this on your right go past a pylon on your left to a stone stile. Over this stile the path follows the wallside down towards West Field Farm to emerge into a small snicket right besides the farm building. Go round the lefthand side of the building and crossing the farm lane go down the field ahead towards the valley bottom keeping close to the wall on your right. Once through the small gateway at the bottom, turn left and follow the lefthand bank of the River Worth until you arrive at Lord Bridge. Turn right now on the road and climb the steep hill back into Haworth.

Walk 19

Brow Moor and Black Moor from Haworth

Grade—Moderate (boots required).
Distance—6 miles.
Time—2½—3 hours.

O N the other side of Bridgehouse Beck the village of Haworth
sprawls on the steep slopes of Haworth Brow. This part of the
village seems to be totally detached from the old world setting on
the west side of the valley, and provides rows of dwelling houses,
where work people employed at the local mills lived. At the top of
the slope is an open heath called Brow Moor, the property of the
Craven Water Board. Indeed, a notice on it proclaims its ownership
but goes on to add that the moor is open to the public, though
camping, lighting fires, caravans and motor cars are strictly forbidden.

If you are entering Haworth from Colne, then proceed on the
main street and cross the river at the bottom, with the Worth Railway
on your lefthand. Instead of following the road round to the left
once over the bridge, turn right and then sharply left, to climb a
steep hill. You will have to stop at the main road, the Hebden road,
but across this a road, signposted Cullingworth and Denholme, takes
you up to Haworth Brow where you will find a convenient car park
on the left opposite the moor.

If approaching from Keighley, then take the left fork at Cliffe Hill,
just beyond a school, signposted to Oxenhope; and at the junction
described above turn left up to Haworth Brow.

Walk down the road from where you have left the car, and then
turn off on to the moor at the first bend. Follow the edge of the moor
overlooking the valley below on your right, until eventually you meet
a narrow metalled road. Go along this road, passing a quarry on
your left and climbing slightly uphill. Beyond the quarry where the
road begins to ease, a grassy track leads off on your right. Go along
this in the direction of the building called Naylor Hill, but do not
turn down to it. Instead follow the wallside on your right to the next
building, passing it on the left to emerge into a grassy lane. Turn left
along the lane and make for the next bend, where a derelict house
stands by some trees. Just past this building on the right, a stile allows
you to follow the contours around the side of the sloping ground and
then makes for a gate to emerge into a muddy overgrown lane. On
your right are ever changing views of Oxenhope and the valley below
as your view point alters.

Here at the lane turn right through a wooden gate and walk down
towards a farm building. In a few yards you will come across a stile
on your left, and the path makes directly for a lane in front of another

Brow Moor and Black Moor from Haworth.

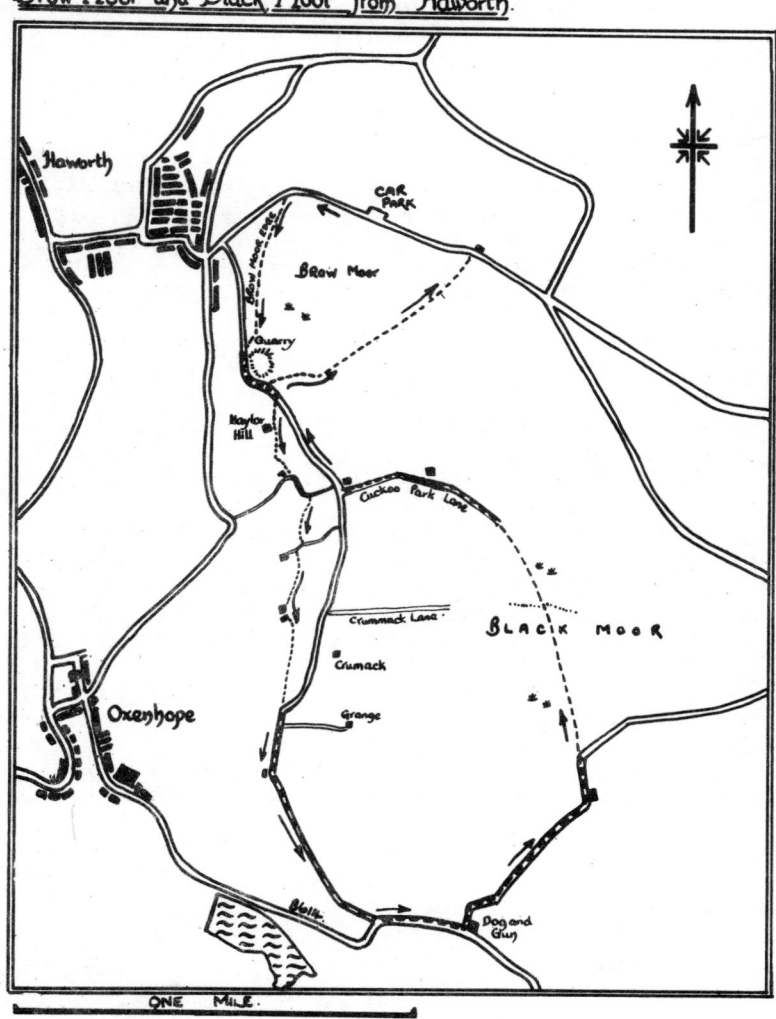

Haworth

CAR PARK

Brow Moor

Brow Moor Side

Quarry

Naylor Hill

Cuckoo Park Lane

Crummack Lane

BLACK MOOR

Crumack

Oxenhope

Grange

Mill

Dog and Gun

ONE MILE.

more prosperous looking farm. Pass this building and go through a stile just beyond it to follow a footpath which climbs diagonally across a sloping heather clad moor to the wall on the skyline.

At this point you emerge on to the road which you follow down the hill until it meets the B614 road leading to Denholme. Turn left here and follow it until you come to the "Dog and Gun" Inn within about 400 yards, and where a road turns off to the left. Turn left and folllow the metalled surface for a good ½ mile, until you come to a sharp efthand bend and a house called Trough Bottom.

Ahead is the open moor, and a path strikes out across it directly from the bend in the road in front of you. Look carefully for the track which is some 10 yards to the right of a natural drainage ditch and follows a compass direction of 356 degrees magnetic. Follow this path, which becomes more pronounced, until you cross the shoulder of the gently sloping moor, to descend to an open gateway in a stone wall.

From here the path continues on a direction of 322 degrees magnetic, later curving to the left and making for two tall trees on the skyline. This is a bleak moor and most aptly named Black Moor with the only sign of habitation ahead beyond the two trees at a place called Cuckoo Park. Here you will enter a lane and following this will bring you to the road besides a farm called Mount Pleasant in about ½ mile.

Turn right on the road and after about 400 yards, on passing a low farm building on your right, look for a corner of a wall. Here a path, just before the quarry, follows the wall on your right towards some trees, and continues along this wallside right across Brow Moor to emerge on the road within a couple of hundred yards from the car park.

Walk 20

Oxenhope, Oakworth and the Worth Valley Railway

Grade—Easy.
Distance—4 miles.
Time—2 hours.

THREE villages, Oxenhope, Haworth and Oakworth are linked together by this walk in order that their exporation be made possible. There is much to see particularly in Haworth, and the return journey to Oxenhope could bring back a nostalgia of a bye gone age if you travel on the Worth Valley Railway.

The Worth Valley Railway is a private company operating the line between Keighley and Oxenhope which was closed by British Rail. This small branch line is now in the hands of steam enthusiasts who have raised money to buy old steam locomotives and renovate them so that they become a working museum of the past. There is a regular weekend service throughout the year, and during the summer months a mid weekly one operates. If therefore you intend to return to Oxenhope by train I would advise that you consult the departure times first.

Park your car at the Worth Valley Railway Station at Oxenhope and leave by the back road clearly signposted to Haworth. About a quarter of a mile from the start as you climb out of Oxenhope, you will come to a modernised old stone building called Moor House. It is situated just above a new housing estate on your right; and here a lane, which soon gives way to a clearly defined path, takes you along the back of the new dwellings towards some farm buildings. Passing through a final stile, turn left into a farm lane and walk up towards the road.

Turn left on the road, and pass on your right a prominent building called Marshlands, surrounded by tall trees. Immediately beyond this, turn right up a side road, and some four hundred yards ahead you will come to an old mill on your left which has been delightfully modernised. At the bend in the road, on your right, is a well kept farm building and the footpath taking you to Haworth begins on the lefthand side of the concreted farm yard. Go through the stile and follow the wallside on your left passing the old Mill Lodge. This path leads in a straight line through a succession of fields, eventually emerging into a lane by the side of some buildings at Hole.

Turn left in the lane and, passing through a gate, make for the bend ahead. Here a stile besides an old fashioned gas lamp leads you in a straight line towards some farm buildings. Turn right at Sowden, over a stile into a narrow pathway constricted on either side by a wall and fence, and follow this as it gently curves round towards the tower of Haworth Church. It soon merges with a broader lane from the left, and proceeds straight ahead for the church building. An iron gate allows access to the graveyard, and passing round the back of the

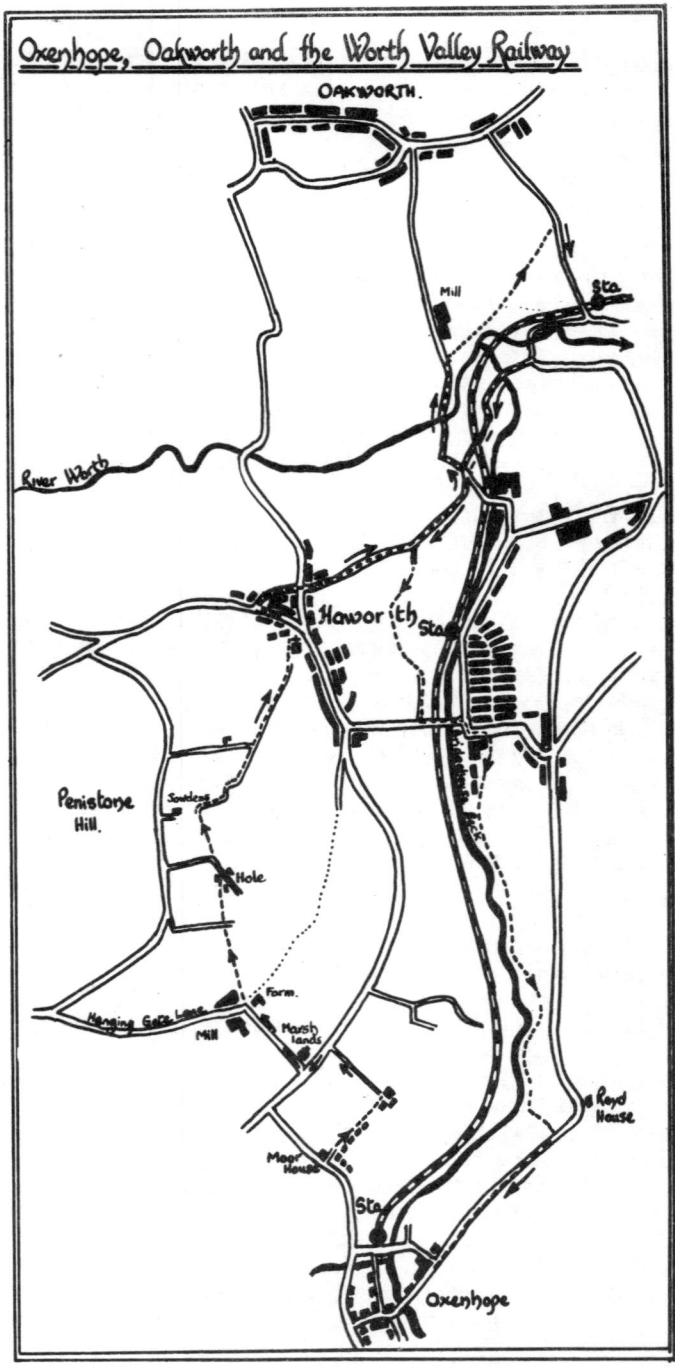

church, you emerge into the cobbled narrow main street of the village.

Turn left and wander along the quaint main street until you pass the new car park entrance on your left. Immediately beyond turn sharply right and follow the road, passing the Haworth Tweed shop and going straight across at the crossroads, to descend in a gradual lefthand curve around the edge of a new housing estate to the bridge over the River Worth.

Ahead the road begins to climb uphill towards Oakworth, and a tall Mill building marks the point where you leave the road. Here some stone steps carry you up to a fenced off lane, which follows the rim of the steep slope dropping, into the river valley on your right. When eventually you arrive at a fork keep straight on and ignore the right hand path leading downhill back towards the river. Soon the lane takes a sharp lefthand turn, and here by a gas lamp, a stile leads you straight across a field to meet the road connecting Oakworth on your left with the Worth Valley Station down the hill on your right.

Just below the station is the Bronte Zoo and some tea rooms which may be of interest, and from here it is possible to make the return journey by rail.

However if you wish to continue, the roads and paths hug the valley of Bridgehouse Beck. Follow the road over the railway crossing and around to the right, passing besides a large mill. The road bends sharply left having passed under a part of the Mill building, and at the second left hand bend, a lane strikes off to the right. Follow this unmetalled surface, crossing a bridge over Bridgehouse Beck just before it merges with the River Worth, and climb up hill until you come to the road which you previously had walked down on the outward journey.

Turn left and walk on the pavement up the hill until you come to the start of a row of houses on the left of the road. Turn left along an unmetalled lane and go through a stile at the bend ahead. Here a path leads across open ground, which rises steeply on your right to the older part of Haworth village, dominated by the church tower on the skyline. Follow the path as it curves gently left, until passing through a gate, it meets a building on your lefthand. Turn left in front of this building and follow the lane which then brings you out onto a street above Haworth Railway Station. Continue along the street, keeping the railway on your left, to the main road ahead.

Turn left over the bridge and follow the road around to the right besides the War Memorial. Ahead is a large Mill building which forces the road to bend to the left. Just around the corner a footpath sign declares that Oxenhope is 1¼ miles distant. This path follows Bridgehouse Beck closely for about 1 mile, crossing two footbridges and various fields, to eventually emerge on to the main Hebden Road just beyond Royd House. The final stretch of the journey follows the main road for a quarter of a mile back into Oxenhope.

Walk 21

Oxenhope, Warley and Ovenden Moors

Grade—Strenuous. boots, map and compass required.
Distance—about 9 miles.
Time—allow about 4½ to 5 hours.

OF all the walks in this book, I think this one gave me the greatest satisfaction. It was long and rough, and in the cool October sunshine the wind whipped my cheeks and sang through the heather underfoot. I strode out across the open landscape with a feeling of well-being, and the worries of the week dropped from me like a cast off piece of clothing. On my right, the waters of Fly Flat Resevoir scudded in white crested foam against the far embankment; and beyond, the rolling moor rose gently to a purple skyline. My only companions were the hill sheep, shaggy in their woollen coats and inquisitive in their looks; and the grouse which flew almost from under my feet with loud protestations at my invasion of their domain.

Close scrutiny of the accompanying map will show that the walk is almost in a figure of eight. This means that about 3 to 4 miles can be lopped off if you wish to shorten the walk by excluding the Rocking Stone Flat section across Warley Moor. It is a pity to miss this out, for this area on a clear day gives the widest variety of views, though the walking is extremely rough.

The approach to the start of the walk is via Oxenhope, and leaving the village travel towards Hebden Bridge along the A6033. As the road climbs out of the village you will pass a church on your right, and come to a zig-zag bend ahead. Beyond this last bend on your left is an unsignposted road. Turn left here and go up the metalled roadway which climbs straight but steeply to Oxenhope Moor. Follow the road until you arrive at a sharp right hand bend which takes you up by the side of Nab Water. On your left a gravel track cuts sharply back wards parallel to the scarp of Nab Hill. Here you can park your car for this is the starting point of the walk.

Shouldering your rucksack, stride out along the road which climbs and curves around the north western edge of Nab Hill. Ahead now is the flat stretch which holds the wide expanse of Fly Flat Reservoir. This large tract of water is used by a Yachting Club, and the fanfare of colour lends an atmosphere of gaiety to the bleaker surroundings.

Continue along the roadway, which is called Cold Edge, and with good reason, for the wind fairly whistles along unhampered by walls

Oxenhope, Warley and Ovenden Moors.

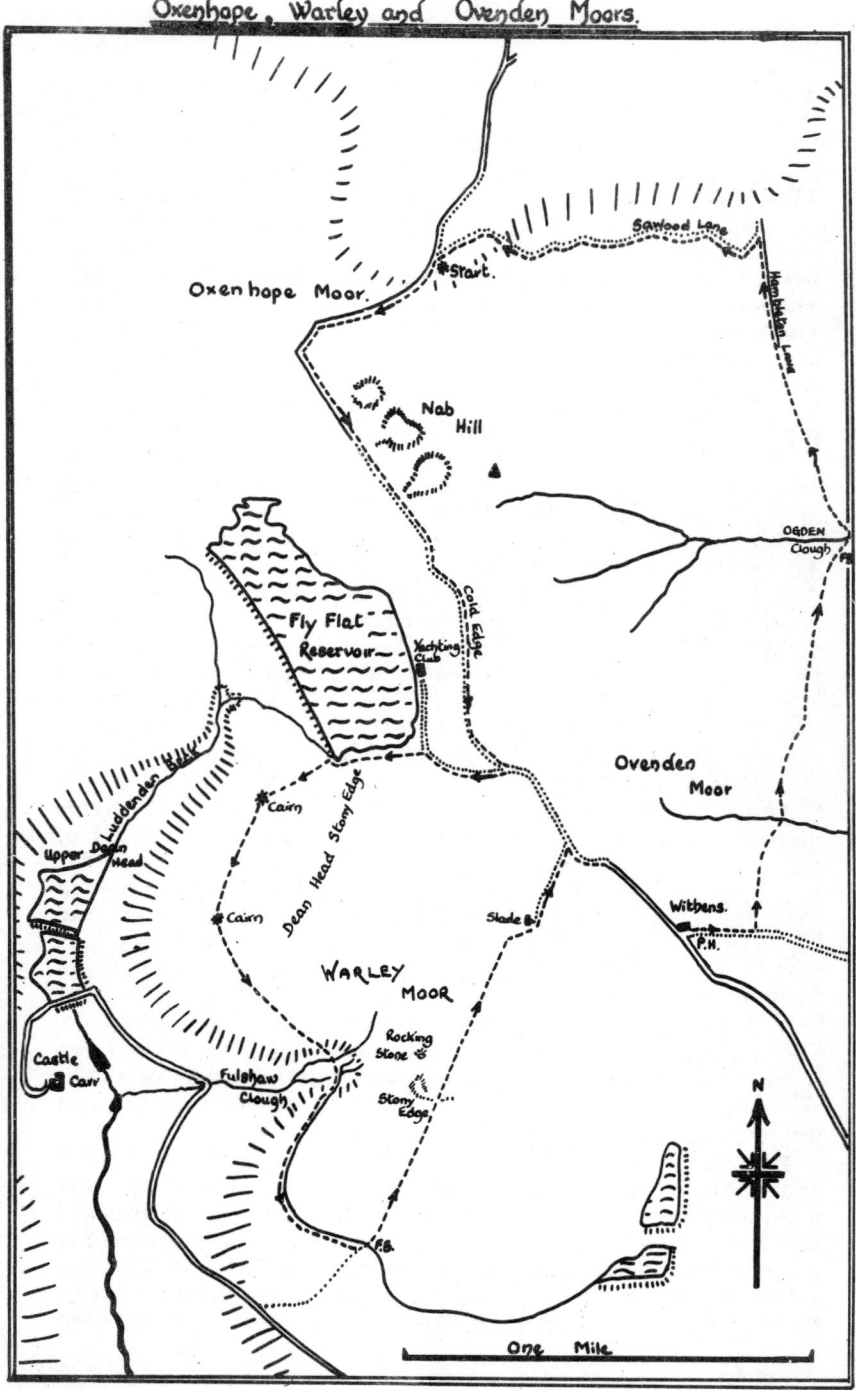

Oxenhope Moor.

Sawood Lane

Start.

Nab Hill

Hey Head Lane

OGDEN Clough

Cold Edge

Fly Flat Reservoir

Yachting Club

Ovenden Moor

Luddenden Dean

Cairn

Dean Head Stony Edge

Upper Dean Head

Cairn

Slade B

Witbens. P.H.

WARLEY MOOR

Castle Carr

Fulshaw Clough

Rocking Stone

Stony Edge

N

F.B.

One Mile

or other barriers. At the end of the reservoir, you will come to the Water Board lane which leads to the water's edge and the Yachting Club. If you continue along the road you will cut out the Rocking Stone Flat section and effectively shorten the walk by about 3 to 4 miles.

Assuming that you will continue, step out boldly towards the reservoir, and where the gravelled roadway curves close to the water's edge, strike off along the lefthand bank of the Reservoir towards the embankment at the south west corner. From this point the path disappears, so set your compass on a bearing of 248 degrees magnetic, which direction will take you directly towards the valley of Luddenden Dean. Tussock grass and boggy conditions impede your progress, but in about quarter of a mile you should pick up a faint track following parallel with the valley beyond.

This track forks at a small cairn, the right hand one descending towards Luddenden Beck, whilst the left hand one follows the rim of the valley. If you look ahead you will notice its progress, for it follows a lighter tract of vegetation bordered on either side by the darker heather. From this cairn your compass direction is 212 degrees magnetic, and follows the lighter patch of tussock grass to another cairn in about quarter of a mile.

On your right is the ever unfolding deep clough of Luddenden Dean with its two small reservoirs and occasional trees. Across this a V shaped cleft rips the hillside beyond, and is aptly named Bare Clough. Above the valley is the outline of High Brown Knoll, crossed by the Limer's Way, the objective of a future walk, and the whole vista is one of magnificence and grandeur.

. At the second cairn reset your compass on a bearing of 136 degrees magnetic to follow the path and lighter vegetation to the head of Fulshaw Clough. The reason for the lighter patch of greenery is due to a water pipeline that follows this path and outcrops from time to time. It leads to the upper end of Fulshaw Clough where the way becomes more evident. Here a water drainage conduit contours around the hillside, and the path follows this a couple of yards to its right.

Now the valley of Luddenden begins to open out, and directly across, you will easily pick out the ruins of Castle Carr at the southern tip of Lower Dean Head Reservoir. Eventually a couple of planks serving as a footbridge cross the conduit, and from here you can follow a compass course of 036 degrees magnetic.

This bearing will take you straight up the slope of Too To Hill and across to a magnificent Millstone Grit Tor called Stony Edge, and directly north of it in a few yards is the perched boulder called the Rocking Stone. Continue along this compass route which follows a line of 6 ft. poles placed at a distance of about 50 yards, until you arrive at a derelict building called Slade. Go round the front of this building and follow the lefthand lane where it forks, to emerge onto the roadway within a half mile of the path leading to the Yachting Club.

Turn right along the roadway and walk along it until you come to a Public House called the Withens Hotel. Go in front of the building, through an iron swing gate and follow an obvious track for about 400 yards, at which point a wicker gate at a notice board allows you to turn left onto the open moor. Here a dual cart-track, along a compass direction of 014 degrees magnetic, is easy to follow and crosses Ovenden Moor.

The track is quite distinct, and in about a mile begins to descend steeply into Ogden Clough. Here a dam holds back the stream and a concrete bridge takes you over to the other side. Immediately across turn left and climb the slope out of the clough and on to the rim of rocks above. Here a track follows upstream, and then after 100 yards turns off on a compass direction of 354 degrees magnetic.

Eventually this path becomes a more distinct lane called Hambleton Lane, and after crossing a conduit the track turns sharply left into another track called Sawood Lane. This final track follows a roughly westerly course for about ¾ of a mile to emerge across White Moor at Nab Water and the original start to the walk.

Walk 22   Cowling Pinnacles

Grade—Easy.
Distance—2—2½ miles.
Time—about 1 hour.

EARL CRAG is the name given to the escarpement which catches the eye of the passing motorist as he drives through Cowling on the Keighley road. It is particularly noticeable, not just for the rocky buttresses, but for the two pinnacles which surmount its crest. Yet how many people, scurrying to and fro and recognising these landmarks, have taken the time to visit them? This walk is a simple excursion to explore the multitude of boulders of Earl Crag, and to visit these man-made memorials.

The pointed spire on the right of the crag from Cowling is called Snowden's Pinnacle and is a memorial erected in memory of Philip Snowden the Chancellor of the Exchequer in the first Labour Government under Ramsay Macdonald. Philip Snowden was born the son of a weaver in Ickornshaw village, and rose through his own efforts to a position of eminence in the land.

The square tower on the left is known as Lund's Tower. It is hollow and a winding staircase spirals up to the battlements above, from which an outstanding view can be obtained of the surrounding countryside.

The starting point of the walk is on the old Oakworth road. As you approach Cowling from Colne, just beyond Cock Hall Bridge a road leaves the main road on the left leading to Ickornshaw village, and opposite Oakworth old road climbs away from Cowling past a church. Turn right and follow the road uphill, turning sharply left after half a mile to come out on to the open moor. Park your car opposite the wall which leaves the road and goes directly towards Snowden's Pinnacle on your left. This is the start of the walk.

Leaving the car, cross the road and follow the wall towards Snowden's Pinnacle which is about 400 yards away. On arrival at the pinnacle scramble on to the rocks so you can see the escarpment to the best advantage, and Lund's Tower about half a mile distant. The boulders here are a natural playground for anyone addicted to simple scrambling. They stand out in disorderly profusion presenting many ledges, excrescences and gullies. The rock is particularly rough, being a typical Millstone Grit, with unusually large crystals of quartzite embedded in the matrix and this helps adhesion when climbing.

Cowling Pinnacles

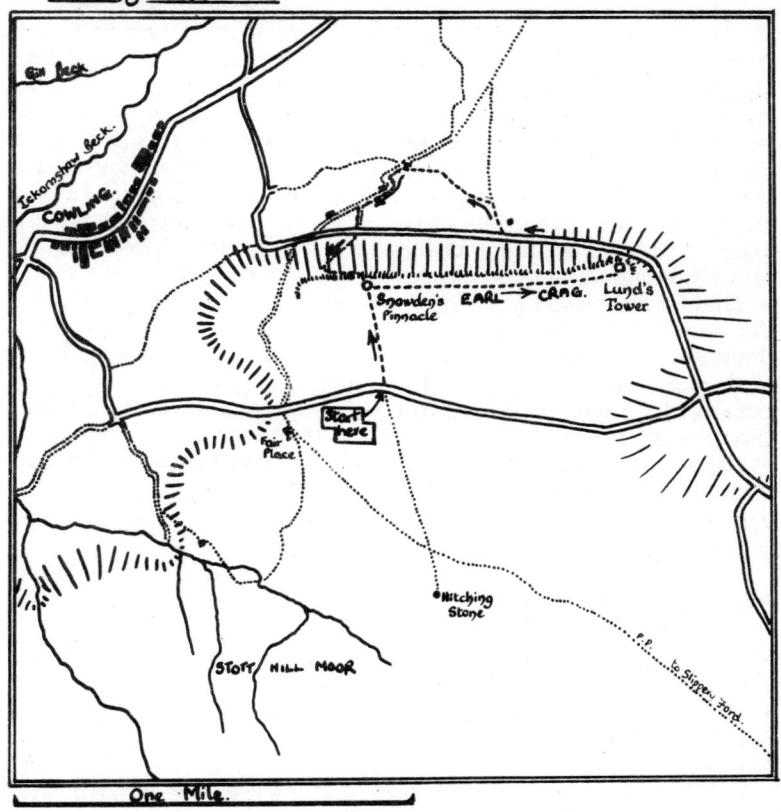

One Mile.

From here turn right and go over a three tiered stone stile and along the edge of the escarpment towards Lund's Tower. Cross a second stile and then later go over a wooden stile to arrive at the Tower. Climb the dimly lit spiral stair and admire the view from the top; then descending walk back to the wooden stile and turn downhill to follow a curving path leading to the road.

On the road turn left and walk downhill in the direction of Cowling for about 300 yards, until you come opposite the farm building on your right. Here a footpath sign reads "Sutton" and directs a way to the right of Brush Farm House. Your path, however, goes straight down to a gateway on the left hand side of the farm building. Here you enter a short grassy lane terminated by a stile. Across this another appears ahead, and a third immediately over the second allows you to cross into a field on your left. The path from here makes diagonally across the field to the opposite bottom corner and from here to the right hand side of the farm called Cragg End Farm.

Pass now in front of the farm building and go through a gate into a grassy lane. A zig-zag bend in the lane leads to the next farm called Summer Seat, and beyond this the lane opens onto rough ground on your left. Make your way now to the road and then select the best possible approach that you can, making for Snowden's Pinnacle. The going here is steep and rough, but on arriving at the rocks a natural gully will be found. This leads from the right hand side of the boulders to just below the Pinnacle, and from here look carefully for a route between two huge boulders with a chock stone overhead to emerge on the crest of the escarpment. From here retrace your steps back to the car.

Walk 23

The Hitching Stone, Slipping Ford and the Pennine Way

Grade—Strenuous. Boots, map and compass required.
Distance—about 9 to 10 miles.
Time—about 5 hours possibly more.

COWLING village is situated on the main Colne-Keighley road, and is over shadowed by the scarp of Earl Crag. Surmounting this rocky excrescence are two man-made pinnacles which can be seen for miles around; but what is not realised by many passers by is that a more natural landmark exists. This is situated behind Snowden's Pinnacle on the open moor, and consists of a gigantic Millstone Grit boulder known as the Hitching Stone. Its very presence on the open moor with no other rocks in sight poses a question. How came it there? Is it a glacial erratic left perched in its present position when the ice retreated? Or, has it been rolled there by the snout of some glacier? Or, has it simply been tossed there a by witch, according to local folklore, as suggested to me by a farmer with a merry twinkle in his eye. Whatever its origin, it is certainly a land mark and well worth a visit.

If approaching from Colne, turn off the main road before entering the village, to the right at Cock Hall Bridge, up a secondary road, signposted "Oakworth". From Keighley it is wisest to pass through the village to emerge by a sharp left hand bend. On your left now is the turn off referred to in the preceding sentence. Follow the Oakworth Old Road, turning sharply left after climbing for about half a mile, and continue along the lane until you come to the open moor on either side. Here a farm on your right called Fair Place, at a point known as Scar Holes, is the starting point of the walk.

Right from the start it is as well to use a compass and tread warily on boggy ground. Though a public right of way exists, it has been so seldom used that no trace of the path remains, and the route to Slippery Ford is an arduous undertaking.

Go through the gate at Fair Place Farm and in the next 20 yards strike out to your left along a natural depression in the sloping moor, on a compass course of 130 degrees magnetic. This bearing points your way up the gentle slope of Round Hill, and once over the ridge descends to a flat boggy stretch. Follow a drainage ditch on your right until you meet a wall crossing your path. On your right looms the Hitching Stone and you should follow the wall up towards it.

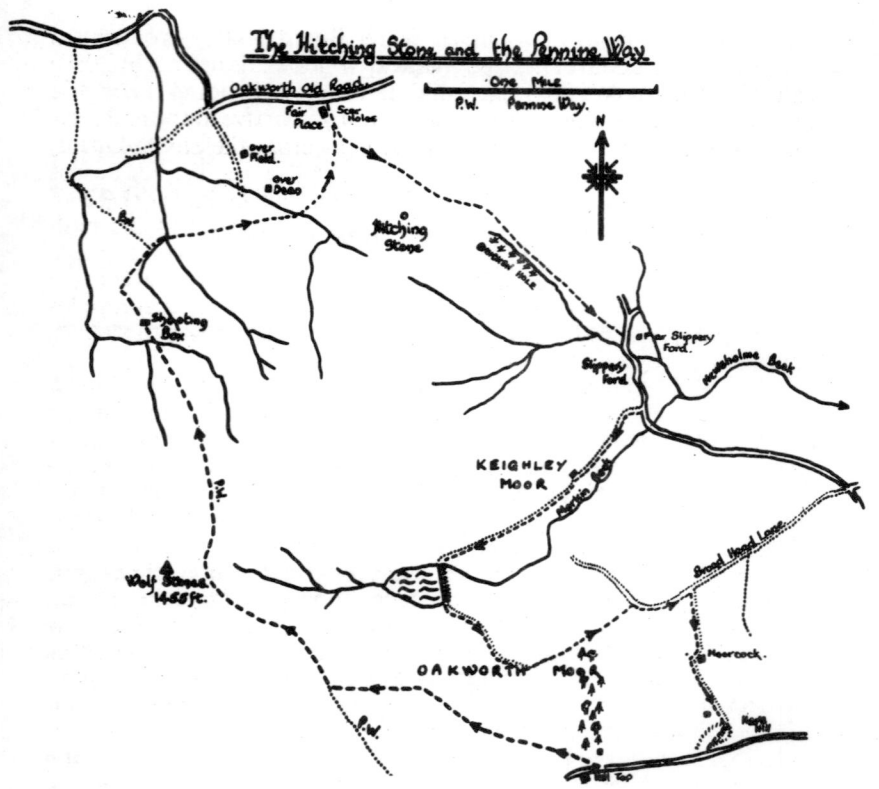

Inspect it closely, and scramble up its sides, for what man can resist the adventure of this private Matterhorn?

Now cross the low wall which strikes out in an easterly direction from the boulder, and follow a compass course of 084 degrees until you drop down to a small stream flowing away from you, Cross over to the other side, and follow it on a course of 134 degrees along the remains of a faint track. This is Slatesden Clough, and the path keeps to higher ground, where it flows across a broad boggy valley known as the Quicken Hole. Cross the wall ahead, and continue on the lefthand bank, descending now towards Slippery Ford.

The path bears to the left, leaving the clough, as it approaches a wall. Look carefully for a stone stile, and once over it, turn left and follow the wall around the very wet area of rushes and bog. Turn right at the corner of the field, and walk alongside the wall towards Slippery Ford. Cross a small beck and go through a wooden gate into another field which you should cross diagonally to the right to emerge on to the road at Far Slippery Ford by a stile next to a gate.

Turn right on the road and walk down the hill to a bridge. On your right here a Keighley and Craven Water Board Notice proclaims a footpath along a dual concreted roadway which leads up to a building called Lower Intake. Pass this building on the left, going through a gate, and continue along the roadway until you arrive at the embankment of the dam. The footpath turns left across the embankment, and on the other side follows a bearing of 146 degrees. It leads across the open moor towards some shooting butts, but make for the wall however to the left of these. A stile takes you over, and the path crosses another line of shooting butts on a direction of 064 degrees. After about three quarters of a mile of rough moorland walking on the compass course stated you will come to a line of telegraph poles and a lane. Turn right along it and pass from the moor through a gate into a broad cart-track called Broad Head Lane.

At the first gateway on your righthand go into a field and follow the fenceline on your left to a derelict building ahead called Moorcock. Pass this on the lefthand side, and going throughan open gateway cut diagonally across the next field to a gap in the wall in the opposite corner. Here you will find yourself on a well defined track which leads over to Hare Hill and the Colne-Oakworth road.

Turn right along the road and walk for a distance of about quarter of a mile along its metalled surface. Soon you will approach two buildings on your right set back on the moor from the road and near to a copse of mixed trees. Here a distinct gravelled roadway leads off to the right passing the buildings and the wood. Ahead this roadway peters out into a rough path which crosses a wooden stile, and follows close by the wall. Because of the nature of the terrain it will probably become necessary to make minor detours, or you will be sure to end up with wet feet. The path continues to follow the wallside on the left and after about 1½ miles from the road it meets another well trodden track merging with it from the left. This is the Pennine Way which goes on to cross one of the rougher sections on its route called Ickornshaw Moor.

Turn right and follow the wall on your left uphill and then across open moor with the occasional cairn as your guide. A Triangulation point on your left marks the high ground of the Wolf Stones, but the track forks to the right missing it out. Once across the summit of this peat and bog desert, the track which must be followed very carefully, begins to descend. Eventually a stone built shooting box will be seen, and the path makes directly for it. Beyond this building the Pennine Way descends alongside a wallside decorated by wooden weekend chalets. However once at the first of these chalets take a compass bearing of 076 degrees and follow the edge of the moor across Dean Moss to the top of Dean Brow Beck, threee quarters of a mile away. Here you will meet a path which follows a wallside round the head of the beck, passing some gigantic flat stones. The path then turns gradually northwards and heads back to Fair Place Farm at Scar Holes.

Walk 24

Foster's Leap and
Lumb Spout from from Wycoller

Grade—Moderate.
Distance—about 5-6 miles.
Time—allow about 2½ hours.

WYCOLLER, a oncepr osperous little hamlet, has been slowly falling into decline over the last few decades. The remains of Wycoller Dean is a direct link with the Brontes figuring as Ferndean Manor in "Jane Eyre", and its ruins remind us of its former prosperity. Today renewed structural activity and renovation work is restoring the decaying buildings, and attracting residents to this natural beauty spot.

It is here that the walk starts. Park your car conveniently in Wycoller and crossing the narrow pack-horse bridge ascend the stone steps ahead and to the left of the ruins of Wycoller Dean. Cross the stile at the top of the bank and follow the line of flagstones erected on your left as a fence for about 200 yards. At this point a gap in the stone fence allows access for a tractor to cross the field to a stone wall opposite on your right. Go across to this wall and follow it to an open gateway. An obvious track contours round the slope keeping to the valley bottom but your route makes upwards and across to an open stile in another line of flagstones. This stile is followed by another at a higher level and the gradient steepens. From the second stile make your way for a hawthorne tree which stands out like a sentinel on the skyline, and from there to the left-hand corner of a stone wall. Following the wall on your right you will meet a lane which you should go along until you reach a convenient point to make for the rocks ahead and Foster's Leap. The reason for the name becomes apparent when you explore the two giant pillars separated by a 7 foot gap.

Returning to the lane proceed down the hill to the front of the farm and go through the first gateway on your right. Turn left and make your way through an opening in the wall ahead, and then in a straight line for the farm known as Parson Lee. The remains of a stile besides a telegraph pole leads you across Smithy Clough to a grassy Land Rover track.

Follow the track to the left passing Parson Lee and climb a stile besides a gate. The track is clearly defined and takes you gradually upwards for about ½ mile to a further gate. Once through this turn right on to a loose stone roadway which links the Colne-Haworth road with Brink End Farm. Follow this roadway for about 50 yards. It is important to follow closely the wall on your right even when it departs from the roadway. This wall brings you to a very marshy corner of the field; cross the wall at this point into to what was once

Foster's Leap and Lumb Spout from Wycoller

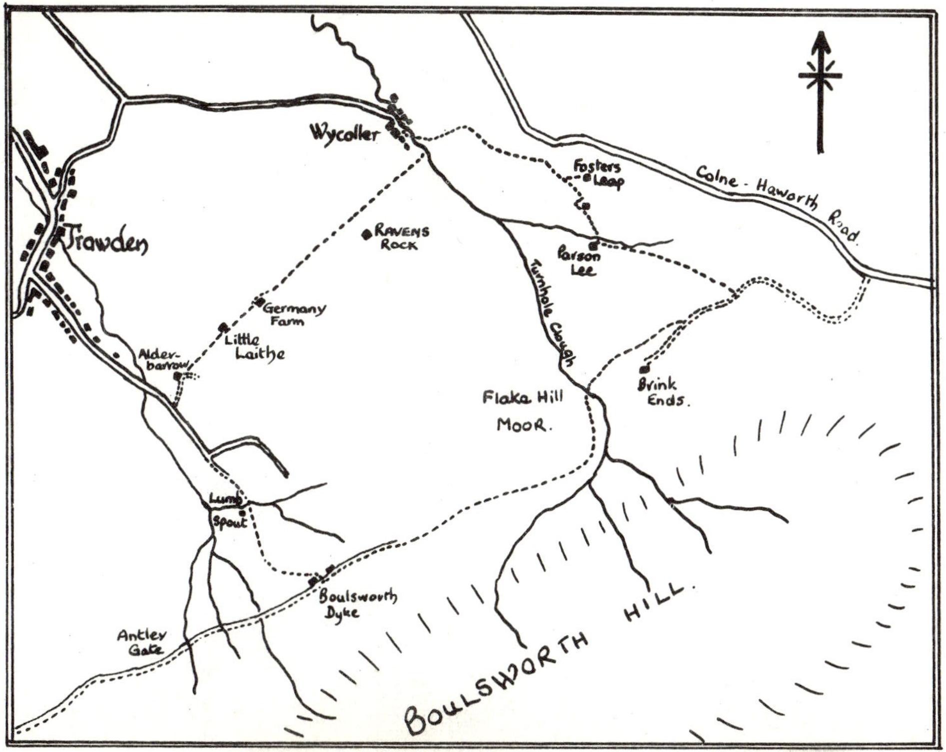

Colne - Haworth Road

Brink Ends

Foster's Leap

Parson Lee

Turnhole Clough

Flake Hill Moor.

Raven's Rock

Wycoller

Germany Farm

Little Laithe

Alder-barrow

Boulsworth Dyke

Lumb Spout

BOULSWORTH HILL

Antley Gate

Trawden

89

a lane but is now a broad drainage ditch full of marsh and bog. On your left is a wall which you should follow, keeping out of the marshy area by walking parallel to it about 10 yards distant. Continue in this direction for about $\frac{1}{2}$ mile.

Ahead you will see a wooden door with a very large white painted arrow on it acting as a swing gate. This indicates clearly your route which then passes into a rough pastured field diverging before you and begins to descend into Turnhole Clough.

On your left higher up the hillside is Brink End Farm, and the path picks its way across marshy terrain following the wallside on your left to finally pass through a gate and cross the stream.

Once across Turnhole Clough, the path, now quite narrow, curves upwards to the left round the shoulder of the hill and then gradually eases to the right around the edge of Flake Hill Moor. Within $\frac{1}{4}$ mile from the stream a wall is reached and followed for about a mile. Eventually two buildings quite close together appear and the second one at Boulsworth Dyke is the next turn off on your route.

Go through the gate and cross the farmyard to pass through a second gate into a rough pasture. Follow the wall on your right hand until you meet a stile some 300 yards distant from the farm. Cross this and make your way diagonally across the field in the direction of Whernside on the skyline and alongside some telegraph poles. The path now begins to drop down towards a stream with a concrete bridge across it and a ruined bungalow on its left.

At this point a slight detour, to the left of the ruin and down amongst the trees, will disclose Lumb Spout; an impressive little waterfall of which the locals of Trawden are justly proud.

Returning to the bridge, a distinct unmetalled road leads to some farm buildings, and from here a metalled surface directs you towards Trawden. About a quarter of a mile from the beginning of the metalled surface you will see a lane on your right labelled "Alderbarrow." Go up this lane and past the building on your left, aiming for a gate where the lane turns sharply towards some outbuildings. Go through the gate, straight up the hill and, eventually when the gradient eases, the building of Little Laithe appears ahead.

The stile is just to the right of the building and the path runs in a straight line all the way back to Wycoller. Follow the line of telegraph poles with a wall on your left until you reach Germany Farm. Go through a small indistinct stile to pass in front of the farm and pick up an unmetalled lane on the other side of it. Keep straight on when this lane takes a turn to the left and follow the wall and then a fence on your righthand. You will now pass through two wooden stiles very close together to meet a wall which you follow in the same direction as before. Raven's Rock Farm is over the wall on your right, and ahead another stone stile takes you into a rough pasture which descends along a wallside into a lane leading you back into Wycoller village.

Walk 25   Hardcastle Crags from Slack Top

Grade—Easy.

Distance—just over 4 miles.

Time—allow yourself at least 2 hours as you will probably want to linger.

THIS is a most popular and delightful walk deserving special mention. However, it is not a walk where scenery can be enjoyed for the path follows the close confines of the river guarded on either side by the steep well wooded slopes of the "Crags". It is best, therefore, to leave this walk until autumn, when the various tints of the leaves give an added dimension to the surroundings, as the shafts of October sunlight pierce the patchwork canopy overhead. It is then, and then only, that the charm of the woodland can be best appreciated.

For many generations it has been the favourite picnic spot of Sunday School outings. Families of local weavers from the nearby cotton towns of Lancashire, and woollen workers from the West Riding descended on it, to bring their children to romp in the stream and explore the woodland paths.

Being accepted as one of nature's playgrounds a huge cry was raised when a scheme was proposed to drown the "Crags" in order to create a new reservoir. The pressure brought to bear by organised protest eventually prevailed and the "Crags" were saved.

I have chosen to start the walk from Slack Top rather than from Hebden Bridge as car parking here presents no problem, and there is ready access by various paths. Park your car on some spare ground at the village of Slack, close to where the road forks to the left to Burnley and to the right to Widdop and Nelson.

Walk along the righthand fork towards Widdop and look out for a stile on your right situated about ¼ mile away, and just past a paved lane which leads off the road on your left. From the stile, the path follows the wall on your left down through two fields to the top of the wooded kloof. Here another stile is the gateway to a path that descends obliquely across the steep contours by a series of stone steps. Plunging ever downwards beneath the trees, the path appears to be never ending, but eventually it merges with a broader one that descends more gradually and brings you to Gibson Mill.

No doubt the footpath was used by the workers of the Mill in a byegone age, when their metal shod clogs clattered to work at 6 a.m., and clumped wearily uphill of an evening to their dwellings at Slack.

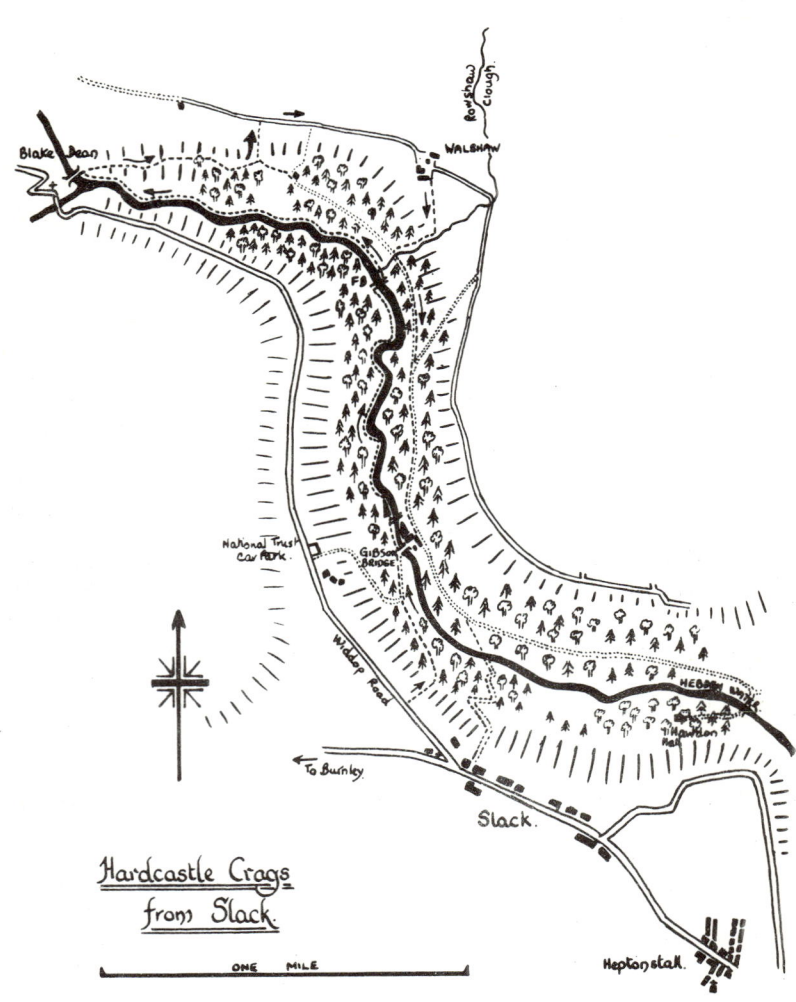

Rowshaw Clough.

WALSHAW

Blake Dean

National Trust
Car Park.

GIBSON
BRIDGE

Widdop Road

HEBDEN BRIDGE

New Bridge
Hall

To Burnley

Slack.

Heptonstall.

Hardcastle Crags
from Slack.

ONE   MILE

Gibson Mill and its surrounding buildings are worth looking at more closely. At weekends in summertime one of the cottages serves as a cafe to trippers, whilst just across the bridge a small narrow building still has a notice pinned to its wall which reads.

Toll Charges.	2 horses and 1 vehicle	6d
	1 horse and 1 vehicle	3d
	Horse and Cow	1d
	Pig and Sheep	½p per head
	Motor Vehicles	6d
	Motor cycles	3d

Retrace your steps back across the bridge to where the path brought you down to it; and follow the path which goes upstream on the lefthand bank. Within a few yards the Mill Lodge will become apparent on your right, and when the lighting is suitable this is a good photographic vantage point from which to snap the Mill.

In two hundred yards or so the path crosses the embankment of the upper Lodge and curves round the righthand side of it. It now leads to Hebden Water and follows the lefthand bank closely for almost a mile. Here are captivating views of ponds ad small cataracts cascading over steps of millstone grit amidst the gentle murmur of foliage stirring in the breeze. Many are the spots where you will linger to examine a flower, to listen to the stream, to capture a view on film and to appreciate the simplicity and solitude.

Some time later, when your mile is almost completed, a small stone building appears, and where the river shallows a well made wooden bridge crosses to the other side. Once across the bridge follow the track which still meanders closely with the river, crossing a tributary stream and eventually emerging from the belt of trees after another delightful mile.

The path still besides the river bank brings you now in ¼ mile to the confluence of two streams: Alcomden Water draining from the north and from the west Graining Water. Together they give birth to Hebden Water which officially starts at Blake Dean. The wooden seat close by the footbridge marks the half way stage in the walk and probably is the most convenient spot for a picnic.

The return route starts directly from the footbridge where a distinct path rises out of the river bed to the rim of the valley. From here the length of the Crags is set out before you though shrouded in trees. Ahead a public footpath sign directs your way, for a second path here diverges taking you back towards the river. Follow the left hand track and make for the trees which are ahead of you at this point. At the top left hand corner of the wood an open gateway allows you access to a path which follows the wallside closely on your left. On your right the land drops steeply away to the river bottom below, and as you enter the trees the distant views are blotted from your vision.

In a quarter of a mile, the trees thin out and the track emerges into an open space. Ignore the stile over the wall on your left, and do not begin to descend even though the track makes down to the remains of a building called Over Wood. Instead continue along the wallside on your left making for the corner where the trees meet the wall. Here a stile crosses the wall into a field and the path takes a diagonal route crossing a second field into a lane. Turn right along the lane and walk towards Walshaw Dean, the buildings ahead, and about ¼ mile distant.

On entering the square between the buildings turn right and go to the lefthand side of the cottage ahead. Here a stile leads you through a field, and on the righthand side of a wall, to the top of the wood. A distinct track follows the course of the stream, Rowshaw Clough, down, sometimes quite steeply, until it emerges through a wooden swing gate onto a broad path. Turn left on this path and follow it for approximately ¾ mile back to the buildings at Gibson Bridge.

Go over the bridge and immediately in front of you a small track begins to climb over stone steps in a winding fashion and quite steeply. Follow this route everlastingly upwards until it meets a broad track near the rim of the crags. Turn right along this lane and follow it, emerging from the trees, to follow a wall which brings you out at the National Trust Car Park. From here walk the final half a mile along the road back to Slack and your car.

Walk 26   Walshaw Dean, Lumb Bridge and Crimsworth Dean

Grade—Easy.
Distance—between 4 and 5 miles.
Time—about 2½ hours.

HARDCASTLE CRAGS is a veritable warren of footpaths which crisscross beneath the overhanging boughs of the mixed hard and soft woods clinging tenaciously to the steep slopes of the clough. Following any of these paths will reveal the solitude and charm of the woods, where dappled shadows and shafts of sunlight alternate in a patchwork of colour. The walk, once you have climbed out of the clough, yields a splendid · panorama of the Crags: the harsh bleak moor and stark fields contrasting strongly with the softer character of the valley.

From the centre of Hebden Bridge take the Keighley road, and driving for about ½ mile up the steep slope, you will come to a road sign on your left marked "Midge Hole and Hardcastle Crags ½m". Take this lefthand fork which drops down to the river, and after passing Midge Hole, crosses a bridge over Crimsworth Dean Directly in front of you are the Lodge gates and a National Trust Car Park on your right. This is the start of the walk.

At the back of the car park in the corner nearest to Crimsworth Dean a path leads into a lane. This curves upwards and to the left, to emerge on to a metalled roadway. Directly opposite, an open area covered by overhanging boughs makes a delightful picnic spot. Cross this and make for a path which takes you up to a tall pylon on your right. Here you will discover a paved lane which passes between two open fields to an afforested belt ahead. Once in the treeline again, the path is quite distinct and follows the wall on your left. It then begins to climb by a series of stony steps, across the contours, until it emerges from the trees by some huge boulders at what is known as Willow Gate. Go over a stile here to follow a narrow lane, between two walls, to arrive at the small hamlet of Shackleton.

Turn left along a roughly paved cart track, which is followed for the next two miles until you enter Walshaw. This track skirts the edge of the escarpment passing Owlers Farm, Mansfield House and Lady Royd. Below is an excellent view of the Crags and woods, whilst across the valley is the village of Slack, and beyond the finger

Walshaw Dean, Crimsworth Dean and Lumb Bridge.

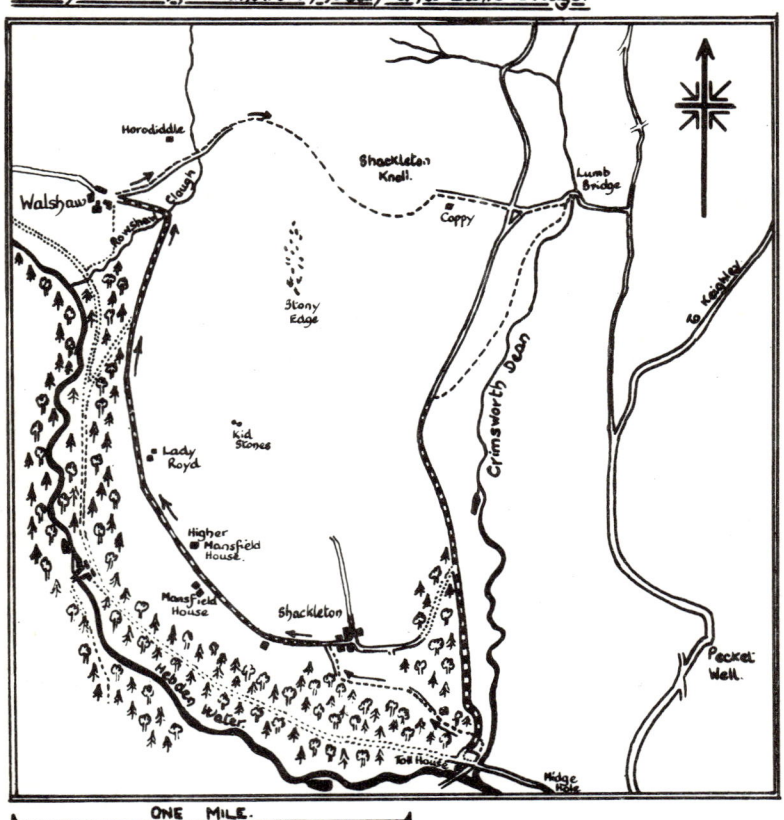

ONE MILE.

of Stoodley Pike stands out clearly on the horizon. From Lady Royd the hamlet of Walshaw can be seen directly ahead.

The walk does not actually enter this ancient cluster of homesteads, but it is well worth while making a detour to examine the architecture and layout of the farm buildings.

On approaching the first building at Walshaw you will notice that a lane cuts back obliquely on your right, and is marked by a footpath sign. This is your route. Pass through the gate and make your way along an extremely muddy lane for about 100 yards, before emerging into an open field. On your left is a farm rejoicing in the unusual name of Horodiddle. Make for the open gateway ahead, and then cross Rowshaw Clough, going through a gate and making for a distinct path which follows the wall on your left.

The path curves slowly uphill and round to the right, then as the gradient flattens out it rounds the end of Shackleton Knoll on your left. Here you find a gate and on the other side a sign reads "Private —Keep out!" Go through the gate and towards the sign, then turn right to follow the track which runs parallel with the wall on your right. The sign denies access to Shackleton Moor which is a grouse moor belonging to the Saville Estate, but the path you are on is a Public Right of Way.

Follow the wall for approximately $\frac{1}{4}$ mile until eventually you come to a gate. This allows you to enter a grassy lane which takes you directly down the hill. You will pass a ruin on your right and approach another derelict building towards the end of the lane. Here turn right through a gate, and then immediately make your way down the hill to your left, to a lane some 50 ft. below you. This lane descends directly to Lumb Bridge.

Having visited the Bridge return up the lane to the first bend where two empty gateposts about 3 feet across denote the start of a footpath which follows a wall on your right. Continue along this footpath on a parallel course to that of Crimsworth Dean below on your left, to cross a stile, followed by an open hillside leading to a second stile. Ahead is a building, turn left down some steps and pass in front of it to a grassy lane. Go through the gate and climb the steepish slope to meet a wide unmetalled road. Now follow this downhill until it eventually brings you back to the Lodge gates and the car park.

Walk 27   Alcomden Water and Widdop Moor from Blake Dean

Grade—Strenuous. Boots are required and it is advisable to carry a map and compass.
Distance—about 5 to 5½ miles.
Time—allow about 3 to 3½ hours as there is some very rough walking.

O NE important geographical feature will have become apparent to any walker in Bronte country. The area is a vast high plateau of acid moor into which streams have carved deep V shaped valleys called Cloughs. These steep sided cloughs often have been used as sites for reservoirs serving the neighbouring industrial towns of the West Riding. Some are wooded, some are bare, but all have character.

At the head of the clough known as Hardcastle Crags, at the confluence of Graining Water and Alcomden Water, stands Blake Dean. Here the road climbs out of the clough by a series of twisting hairpins, and at this point is the site of a small Baptist chapel and its adjoining graveyard. No longer used as a house of worship, it now serves as a Hostel for visiting Scout Troops. The road is sufficiently wide here to draw your car close to the wall and leave it.

Walk down the sloping road to a lane which is closed to the public by a strong iron barred gate. Besides this a stile takes you over to the twin concreted track which curves around the hillside. It follows Alcomden Water upstream on your right, yielding magnificent views of the deep V shaped cleft, which gradually flattens out, on your approach to a barn and bridge carrying a Land Rover track over towards Walshaw. From here the metalled roadway climbs slightly and the embankment of the Lower of Walshaw Dean reservoirs comes into view, backed in the distance by the impressive barren moorland of Withens Height.

Where the road forks, take the right hand one, and in a few yards it merges with a main roadway leading to the Reservoir Lodge. This pathway is the Pennine Way tramped by many, ambitious to complete the 270 miles of its length. For half a mile you follow this sacred way, until, nearly at the end of the first reservoir, you see a shallow gully descending to it from your left. Here a sign post proclaims your route over a private footpath crossing the Saville Estate.

Read the notice carefully, and as long as no flags are flying, set off for the wall about 50 yards distant from the Pennine Way. You are now committed to some of the most difficult walking it will ever be

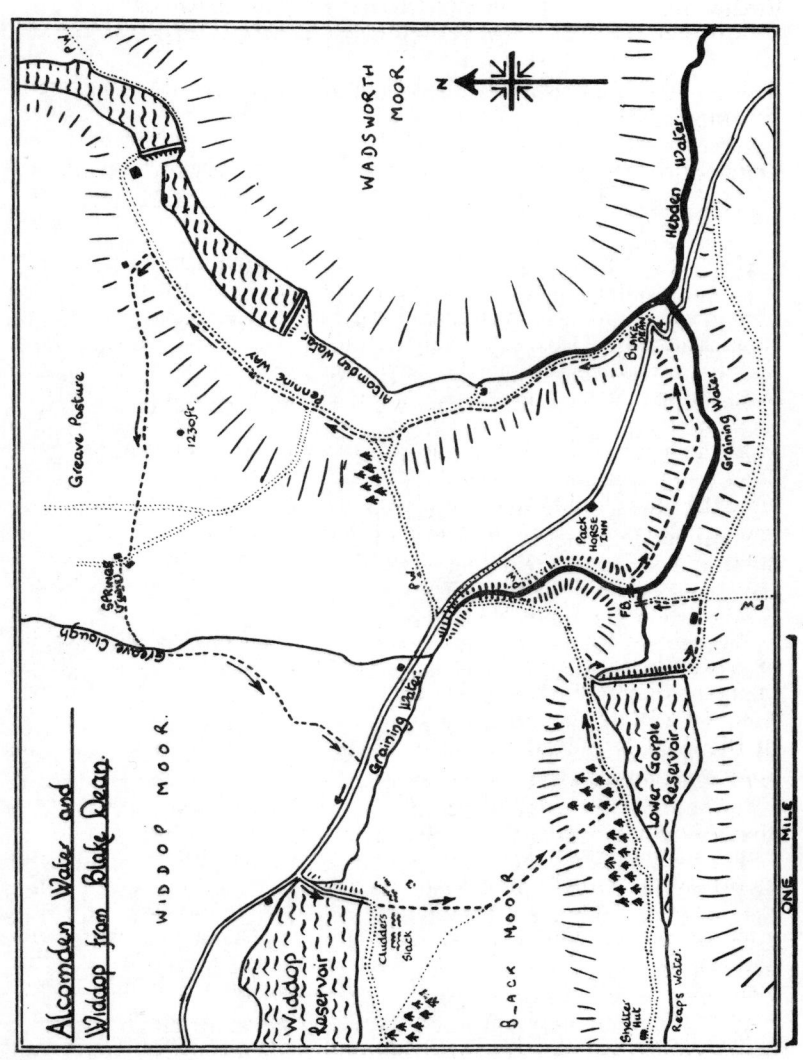

Alcomden Water and
Widdop from Blake Dean.

WADSWORTH MOOR

N

Hebden Water

Alcomden Water

Pennine Way

Greave Pasture

1230ft

Graining Water

Pack Horse Inn

F.B.

Md

Greave Clough

Greaves
Cross

Lower Gorple Reservoir

Graining Water

WIDDOP MOOR

BLACK MOOR

Cludders Slack

Widdop Reservoir

Smelter Hut

Reaps Water

ONE MILE

99

your lot to meet. Indeed, I can' assure you, that no stalwart on the Pennine Way will have to cross anything more strenuous, so take your time, use a compass and take care.

Once through the gap in the wall, the footpath, if you can find one, follows parallel with the wall, gradually climbing until ahead you see the mounds of debris from a once worked quarry. Make for the right hand side of the quarry rubble, and from there set 276 degrees on your compass and follow it across what is called Greave pasture.

On your left you will see a wall and Triangulation point about 200 yards away marking a height of 1230 ft., and ahead you will see a fence line. Still on the same compass course (276 deg. magnetic) make for the righthand end of the fence, and then follow it on your left as the ground begins slowly to descend. Eventually a Land Rover track crosses your path at right angles, and from here you can make directly for some ruins and four tall trees ahead.

You will now meet another track which leads right into the trees, and between the skeletons of two buildings. Follow this track until it begins to turn right after leaving the proximity of the trees. Here a faint double wheeled track detaches itself, and makes for a gap in a wall, by the side of a solitary gatepost. Beyond this is Greave Clough, and the track curves slightly left, heading for the end of a wall by the steep embankment.

Below you at this point is a weir or dam, no doubt man's efforts to prevent sudden flooding in times of cloud burst. Descend the steep slope and cross the stream below the dam. Turn left and make for the wooden stile over the wall. Though it is still difficult terrain, there now exists a distinct path which passes through a gorge. The path maintains its height whereas the stream continues to fall leaving rocky Millstone Grit Tors outcropping and yielding impressive scenery.

The path emerges from the clough and curves right through deep bracken crossing a small tributary stream close by a filter bed, built no doubt to purify the water supply of the farm house downstream. Continuing in the same direction, the track meets the main Widdop road besides a similar notice declaring the Saville Estate's rights.

Turn right along the road and walk towards Widdop reservoir about ¼ mile distant. On the left, Widdop rocks, known as Cludders Slack, stand out against the skyline, and on top a curious Millstone Grit boulder shaped like a sugar loaf catches your eye. When you arrive at the iron gate to cross the embankment, a footpath sign reads "Gorple 1m, Worsthorne 3½m".

Cross the embankment and at the end begin to climb the steep gully to the right of the second buttress from the left. A pause here to explore the various rock shapes will give you some idea of the domain of the rock climber; and should you be walking at weekend, it is more than likely that some will be practising their craft on the vertical gritstone.

At the top of the gully is the open moor and if you set your compass on 178 degrees magnetic and walk on this course, you will eventually meet a Water Board road running parallel alongside Lower Gorple Reservoir. The walking here is strenuous in the extreme, and requires care to negotiate the tussocks, which continue for about ½ mile, before emerging between two areas of conifers onto the road.

Turn left and walk along the twin concreted roadway, until you reach the embankment of Lower Gorple Reservoir. Here follow the road across towards the Water Bailiff's house, and round the back of it. Just beyond the house on your left a path leads down towards Graining Water. This is the Pennine Way and is signposted by a yellow acorn motif.

Follow this path and steeply descend the stone paved staircase down to the confluence of Graining Water with the stream which comes from Lower Gorple Reservoir. Go across both of the footbridges and instead of turning left and following the Pennine Way, turn right and make your way up hill to the stone wall on your left. The path follows close by the wall, and then leaving it, goes in a straight line to emerge at Blake Dean on the hairpin bend directly opposite the Chapel.

Walk 28

Reaps Cross and the Pennine Way from Colden

Grade—Moderate, some strenuous walking.
Distance—about 5 miles.
Time—about 2½ hours.

THE site of Reaps Cross is probably an old monastic landmark which leads a number of footpaths from one valley to another by the easiest gradient. Little is left of the cross, but it is worth visiting, for on a clear day the views are an ample reward for the hardwork involved in reaching it. It is a bleak place, typical of the Millstone Grit Moors, and to reach it by the proposed route involves some hard walking along a part of the Pennine Way.

The most convenient parking place is at the New Delight Inn where Jack Bridge spans Colden Water carrying the Burnley-Hebden Bridge road across it. Here the landlord and his wife actually welcome hikers, muddy boots and all, and their hot pie and peas have often taken pride of place over my humble sandwiches on a cold weekend.

Leaving the warm confines of the Inn, walk up the road towards the first bend where a stony lane leads off, and a footpath sign guards the way to Hebden Bridge. The lane follows the contours of Pry Hill on your right, and Colden Water frolics along in a steep sided ravine on your left. About 400 yards along this lane you will see a stone bridge crossing the stream. This takes the Pennine Way path across and up to Colden Village. Continue along the lane until you meet a building on your right called Long Row Bottom. Turn left and follow the Pennine Way down to the footbridge.

A few minutes of exploration close by the footbridge reveals the spot as a most delightful picnic place for a hot summers afternoon. Here you can relax and bathe your feet, or explore shallow pools, or scramble among the rocks, or just sit contemplating the solitude; for it is a place for meditation.

Cross the picturesque bridge and turn right under the leafy boughs to climb steeply out of the ravine by means of a few well placed stone steps. When the steep incline eases, the path enters an extremely muddy and overgrown lane. Pick your way carefully along this morass for the full length of the lane, about 250 yards, then turn left and make for some farm buildings. Pass to the right of these into a broad lane which leads uphill to the Burnley-Hebden Bridge road.

Directly across the road is a stile marked with a little yellow acorn motif, the emblem which signifies the Pennine Way. Cross the field beyond to emerge into a lane by a second stile. Across the lane a narrow path between two stone walls climbs the steep slope using

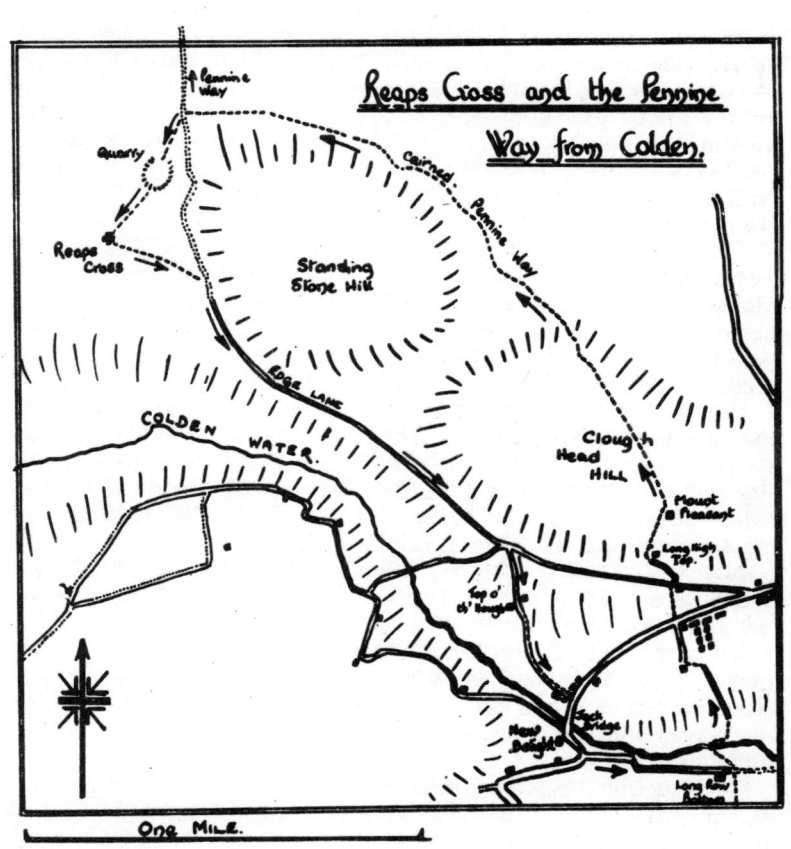

Reaps Cross and the Pennine Way from Colden.

One Mile.

cobbled paving stones as steps, until you emerge on open moor besides the building of Long High Top.

From here follow the wallside on your right which mounts the crest of the hill and begins to descend over the other side to a building called Mount Pleasant. A large stone cairn here marks the point at which you strike out across open moor on your left by a cairned route in a roughly north-north-west direction.

Your direction can be taken by aiming for the top left end of a wall on your right at Clough Head, and about ½ mile distant. The path is now rough underfoot, with unsuspecting potholes and boggy stretches, and it is on this section that you really appreciate the need for a stout pair of boots.

The path, which has now been widened by countless boots trudging along the entirity of the Pennine Way, is always distinct, and cairns are placed at strategic points. It climbs slightly from the end of the wall over the slopes of Clough Head Hill and then contours at the 1200 ft. level for another ½ mile before meeting another wall.

Ahead is Lower Gorple Reservoir, and the land falls away on your right into the valley carrying the stream called Graining Water. In front of the reservoir and further down the hill is the Water Bailiff's house, and the Pennine Way continues along the wallside until it ends and then turning right goes down towards it. It is at this point that your way leaves the Pennine Way, and instead of turning right and going through a gate, it turns left and leads uphill towards Reaps Cross, in a South-South-West direction. Take care here for a faint Land Rover track strikes uphill heading due South and if you follow this you may miss Reaps Cross, though you should be able to see it standing out on the skyline.

The return route is relatively straight forward and leaves the cross on an East-South-East course. The track soon disappears amongst the tussocks so that you are forced to pick your way carefully avoiding boggy sections but travelling in a roughly parallel course to the wall on your right. In about 400 yards your route merges with the Land Rover track. Turn right here and go down to a gate leading into a lane called Edge Lane, and which you follow for approximately one mile.

On your right the land descends to the valley bottom and Golden Water, whilst on your left is the edge of Stony Turgate Hill and its sour acid moorland grass.

After about a mile of travel along Edge Lane you will come to a metalled side road which drops obliquely down to your right. Just beyo nd this, on your right, an overgrown grassy lane, which begins with a narrow wire mesh gate, leads down to a farm known as "Top o' th' Hough". Go down the lane and through the farmyard, to pass through the gate immediately ahead, and follow the broad path in a sweeping curve across the field to the school at Colden. Turn right on the main road, cross Jack Bridge, and head for the New Delight.

Walk 29   The Limer's Way over Midgley Moor

Grade—Strenuous. This is a long and difficult walk crossing mainly open moor where tracks, though Public Rights of Way, are indistinct or have been obliterated through lack of use. A compass and map are essential as is also a stout pair of walking boots.

Time—allow at least 4 hours.

Distance—approximately 8 to 9 miles.

THE return section of this walk goes along an old Pack Horse route called the Limer's Way. Many of these old bridle paths and pack horse trails cross the Pennine moors from West to East, and the one which is walked in this description originates either at Worsthorne or Colne and goes right through to Halifax. It certainly passes Widdop, and follows the line of the present road, passing the Inn to which it gives its name, and from there over to Walshaw Dean. From here it winds over Shackleton Moor, and crosses Crimsworth Dean by means of Lumb Bridge emerging at the A6033 and then following Luddenden Dean down to Mytholmroyd.

One feature which is an all too familiar sight to walkers in Bronte country are the numerous decaying stone remnants of hill farms which flourished before the turn of the century. Wool, required by the extensive Woollen Industry of the West Riding, was the economic livelihood of these proud hardy hill farmers. The life was rough and a constant battle against the elements with the peat moor always threatening to engulf the scanty grass. Lime was used to sweeten the ground and encourage the growth of grass. These routes were congested with strings of pack horses carrying panniers of lime from Clitheroe or Craven to these outlying farms, and this is the reason for the name given to this walk.

In order to get to Midgley, the start of the walk, drive along the Halifax road to Luddenden Foot and there turn off to the village of Luddenden. In half a mile before arriving at the village, a lefthand fork in the road takes you up to Midgley in another half mile. It is a village which sprawls untidily along this road, without a centre and seemingly without a purpose. Here you will have to find a spot to park, which is no easy task, as the road is narrow and space limited. Having deposited your transport make your way to the Co-operative Stores on the bend in the road. Directly opposite, an unmetalled lane leads steeply upwards and this is the start to the walk. Actually at this point two lanes exist which climb uphill side by

Limer's Gate from Midgley.

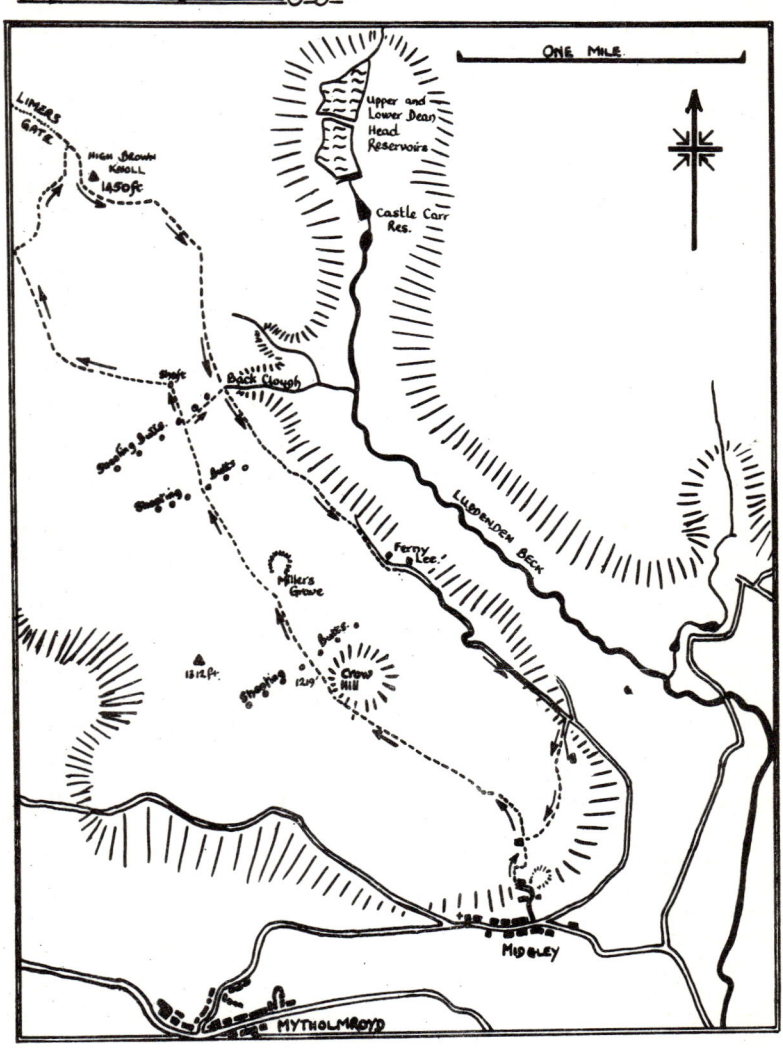

side. Take the right hand one and walking uphill for about 300 yards, follow it round to the left, to pass a row of cottages on your right. At the very end of the buildings a neat stone built stile and swing gate leads into a field. Go straight up the field following the wallside to one of the narrowest stiles it has ever been my lot to squeeze through. Turn right, and walk towards a line of telegraph poles which you must follow up and to the righthand side of a farm building. Mount the steps and pass along the side of the building to emerge through a gateway with the open moor ahead

From here it is as well to have your compass ready and set, even though it may be a fine day, as you never know when a mist might come down. Set a magnetic course of 006 degrees and go up the bank across the heather for about 200 yards. Now alter your compass to a setting of 326 degrees magnetic and follow the path, if you can find one, on this reading. Ahead you will be able to see the rise which is Crow Hill, 1219ft., and which is your first destination. Pick your way carefully and after about 400 yards come round on to a compass course of 306 degrees magnetic which should lead you to the lefthand side of Crow Hill. By all means detour so that you mount the summit for it will help you to set your compass again and spy out the land ahead.

From the summit of Crow Hill the path lies along a compass course of 340 degrees magnetic, and crosses a shallow depression, before beginning again to ascend across the sloping moor. In the hollow, a line of shooting butts lie across your path, and a drainage channel mounts the slopes on the far side. This is the direction of your path.

In the distance on your left Stoodley Pike stands out whilst in the middle distance the line of shooting butts are terminated by a tall singular upright stone. Begin now the rough ascent by the side of the shallow drainage ditch, and with no apparent path take care where you place your feet. After half a mile or so a rough mound will be seen on your right, and this is known as Miller's Grave, though the reason for the name is lost in antiquity. Just beyond, a large boulder on your right acts as a good landmark in this desert of peat and heather.

The drainage channel continues and is quite distinct from now on and should be followed. At this point the upper valley of Luddenden Dean will be evident and the first reservoir at Lower Dean Head. Across the valley on your right are the open moors of Oxenhope and Ovenden which provide a further walk nearer to Haworth itself.

Ahead now, the drainage channel begins to descend slightly as it drops down to a col. Another line of shooting butts remind you that this is a grouse moor, and as you pass them you will see yet another line ahead. Beyond this final line of shooting butts in the base of a depression known as Dimmin Dale is a stone built shaft. Make directly for this.

You now have the choice of cutting the walk short by following a path to your right towards a gate in a wall, or of continuing to the ventilation shaft ahead. If you decide on the former then follow the line of shooting butts until you come to a stream just before you reach the gate in the wall. This stream is called Back Clough and falls steeply down a narrow V chaped cleft to Luddenden Dean below. Here at the stream is the pathway known as the Limer's Way. Turn right and follow a compass course of 152 degrees magnetic to go alongside a wall on your left.

Should you choose to continue, turn left on reaching the ventilation shaft. The path follows an underground drainage system with ventilation shafts every so often. Walk towards the other shaft ahead and when about half way there take a faint track which leads uphill on your right across the moor on a compass direction of 327 degrees magnetic. This at first ascends over rough terrain, crossing a tongue of moorland, and then descends over the brow to the righthand side of some old quarry workings. Here you will meet a broader cart track, and from it you strike out across the rim of the moor on a bearing of 012 degrees magnetic, along what is known as Deer Stones Edge. This track swings round first to the left and then right to mount the slopes of High Brown Knoll to a triangulation point situated in a sea of peat.

The return route starts from here, for at the base of the Knoll the Limer's Way curves around the south facing slope of the Knoll. In front of you and to the east the slope descends rapidly into Lower and Upper Dean Head Reservoirs, whilst to your left, to the North-east is the embankment of Fly Flat Reservoir. Following the path for about 400 yards, it suddenly swings south-west descending and crossing the shoulder of Low Brown Knoll to descend to Back Clough.

The path now crosses the stream at Back Clough and is joined by a private footpath from the left. Follow the wall on your left hand for about ½ mile when the path will become more distinct at Ferny Lee, a desolate ruin that figured in a film on the Brontes recently. On your left are magnificent views of Luddenden Dean, its richly wooded opulence contrasting sharply with the poverty of the moor. The path now is wide enough for a Land Rover and continues as a lane becoming metalled just before reaching a farm called High House.

On your right here is a steep dual concreted track climbing uphill for about 100 yards. Go up and follow the fence line at the top which curves gently right with the open moor on your right hand. Eventually you will arrive at the farm building above Midgley which you passed on your outward journey. Turn left down the side of it and cross the field by way of the telegraph poles. Turn right by a wall and go through the narrow stile. From here you retrace your steps back to the lane and down into Midgley.

Walk 30   Widdop Cross from Swinden Bridge

Grade—Strenuous. Boots are essential.
Distance—about 7 miles.
Time—about 3 hours of walking.

IT will be very noticeable that walking in Bronte country requires greater physical effort than the walks in the softer adjacent Pendleside. Boots are an essential piece of equipment, and because of the terrain a compass and map are wise additions to your rucksack. This walk from Swinden crosses some fo the wilder more desolate moors between Burnley and Widdop, and the weather can make it a delightful or a diabolical undertaking. Driving rain, mist and cold here can make the walk into almost an exercise in survival so choose your day carefully.

Having found a suitable parking spot walk down to Swinden Bridge, the start of the walk. Here a private roadway to Ing Hey lies along the public footpath which is signposted "Thursden 1¼m., Widdop Moor 3m.". Follow the gravel road, ignoring a grassy track leading up to the dam on your right, and when it begins to double round towards Ing Hey, go through a gate ahead. This leads into a small paddock with a cluster of wooden huts, and the exit is by a second gate on to the open moorland.

Once through the gate turn right. Ahead is a quarry whilst the corner of Swinden Reservoir lies on your right. The path is not very clear but makes for a pylon, and then continues at the same level running parallel with the boundary wall of the reservoir. Now begin to cross the contours by climbing gradually on your left to an upper track leading from the quarry. The path, clearer now, leads towards the upper reaches of the valley of Swinden, barren of tree life, and backed by the higher expanse of Extwistle Moor. This is the land of the curlew and lapwing, and even the hardier strains of sheep have difficulty surviving the bleak winters that sweep the landscape bare of succulent grass in favour of the coarse sedge, sphagnum and peat. Eventually as you round the sloping shoulder of the hillside, a wall crossing your path comes into view, and in it you will discern a wooden stile. From here the path follows a narrow channel full of rushes, and climbing slowly curves round the side of the hill known as Delph Hill.

Ahead the scenery changes and Delph Hill becomes pock marked

Widdop Cross from Swinden Bridge

with the slag heaps from an old quarry or mine. The path now climbs more steeply towards the righthand end of the terminal mound, and levelling off and rounding it, makes for an open gateway in a wall.

Once through the gateway it descends steeply on the right to the end of a deep drainage ditch where stones have been placed to bridge the morass of water saturated sphagnum. Follow this drainage channel on your left until you come to a small deep clough where landslip action has carried away the path. Make your way round the top lefthand end cautiously, and then note that the path begins to make more to the left and up the hill in a N.E. direction.

As you curve round the side of the slope on your right, a col or gap becomes noticeable separating the hillside that you are on from that of Delph Hill. This gap becomes more pronounced and is almost like a pass leading from one valley to another. It is known as Middle Edge and leads more directly to Thursden.

Slowly the path mounts the crest of the hill known as Small Edge, and beyond the slopes of Boulsworth stand out against the skyline, bisected by a new ribbon of roadway made by the Water Board. The beginning of this roadway marks the site of Widdop Cross.

Pass a leaning gatepost standing in solitary seclusion amidst a rubble of stones which were once a wall, and make directly for the site of Widdop Cross which should now be in view. Here the road leading from Thursden to Widdop marks one of the higher routeways travelling from Lancashire to Yorkshire.

From the site of the Cross join the road and walk down the slope towards Widdop. Ahead you will see the first house in Widdop and on its right both the reservoir and the grotesque shapes of some Millstone Grit Tors which are the playground of local climbers. Further down the slope a stream, Birkin Clough, drains the area of Small Edge and acts as the County Boundary.

Once over the bridge at Birkin Clough the path strikes out on the right bank of the stream which descends towards the reservoir. There is no evidence of the existence of this path though it is clearly marked as a public right of way on the Ordnance Survey map. Make your way, therefore, as best you can through the rushes and boggy sections to a wall which runs parallel with the right hand side of the reservoir. The footpath follows closely the right hand side of this wall for about ½ mile. climbing slowly away from the reservoir on your left. On your right an escarpment called "The Brinks" looms over your path denying access to the crest.

Eventually towards the end of the wall you will notice a distinct path leading from the Tors, and your path merges with it. Ahead on the skyline are 3 or 4 large boulders and the path zig-zags upwards to them. Once across the crest follow the double wheel marks of a vehicle which curves in a shallow cut roadway and eventually the gradient eases.

111

From this viewpoint you will see the expanse of Worsthorne Moor ahead, with Black Hambleton or your left and Gorple Reservoir in the valley bottom. Directly ahead are the ruins of Gorple Farmhouse and the path makes directly to the righthand side of it.

From here there should be no problem concerning route finding for this broad track leads past Gorple ruins directly into Worsthorne some 3 miles distant. It seems never ending maintaining the same approximate height with occasional ups and downs, and even traversing for $\frac{1}{2}$ mile a section paved with railway sleepers. This section can be treacherous in the wet being greasy and slippy. It is still, however, rough going even though a Land Rover may be met on route, and you can imagine my alarm when in the dark I was once overtaken by a motor cyclist.

Cant Clough reservoir appears on your left, and as you near Worsthorne, Hurstwood reservoir comes into view. Descending now the path makes for the righthand side of this reservoir and after a short spell of uphill walking arrives at a gate. Once through the gate the path becomes a lane, bordered on either side by stone walls, and runs downhill in a straight line into Worsthorne village.

Half way down the hill a barn or cattle shed will be encountered on the right. Here a gate allows you access into a field and a path follows close by a wall on your right making for Swinden. Go through three fields in the same direction and then begin to descend to the left of the reservoir ahead to emerge on the road just above Swinden bridge.